JUNKERS Ju 87
STUKAGESCHWADER
1937-41

AIRCRAFT OF THE ACES: MEN & LEGENDS 21

JUNKERS Ju 87 *STUKAGESCHWADER* 1937-41

OSPREY AVIATION

del Prado publishers

Publisher: Juan María Martínez
Editor-in-Chief: Juan Ramón Azaola
Based on: *Junkers Ju 87 Stukageschwader 1937-41*

Text by John Weal
Cover Artwork by Iain Wyllie
Aircraft Profiles by John Weal
Figure Artwork by Mike Chappell
Scale Drawings by Mark Styling

DISTRIBUTION:

COMAG Magazine Marketing
Tavistock Road
West Drayton
Middlesex
UB7 7QE
Telephone number: 0870 7297999
Subscriptions and back numbers :
WOODGATE
Aircraft of the Aces Subscription Offer
Freepost TN 7153
PO Box 1
Hastings
TN35 4BR
Telephone number: 01424 755577
The price of each part is £ 4.95
(with the exception of No 1 at £ 1.95).

AUSTRALIA
Distribution: GORDON AND GOTCH LIMITED
Subscriptions: WELDON by mail
Reply paid 1900
Aircraft of the Aces Subscriptions
P.O. Box 1900
Mona Vale NSW 1658
Telephone number: (02) 9979 0222
Fax number: (02) 9979 7107
Back issues: These can be ordered through your newsagent, or write to **Aircraft of the Aces**, Gordon and Gotch Limited, PO Box 290, Burwood, Victoria 3125. Please enclose cover price plus A$ 1.50 p&h per issue.

NEW ZEALAND
Distribution: GORDON AND GOTCH (NZ) LIMITED
Subscriptions: WELDON by mail
Freepost 108466
Aircraft of the Aces Subscriptions
P.O. Box 47863
Ponsonby, Auckland 1034
Telephone number: (09) 377 3798
Fax number: (61 2) 9979 7107
Back issues:
Gordon and Gotch (NZ) limited
PO BOX 24013, Royal Oak, Auckland,
New Zealand

SOUTH AFRICA
Distribution: RNA
Subscriptions and back orders:
JACKLIN ENTERPRISES
Private Bag,12
Centurion,0046
Tel.: 011 265 4308
Fax.: 011 314 2984
Subscriptions Email Address:
Subscribe@jacklin.co.za

I.S.B.N (for the whole work): 84-8372-207-0
I.S.B.N (for this volume): 84-8372-445-6

Front cover
Flown by the Staffelkapitan of 5./StG 77, Ju 87B-1 "Anton –Nordpol" (S2+AN) releases its full warload of a single 250-kg bomb and four 50-kg underwing bombs against a target in the western Channel in the high summer of 1940. Moments after dropping its ordnance the Ju 87 was set upon by a Hurricane I of Fighter Command's No 10 Group and badly shot up (cover painting by Iain Wyllie)

CONTENTS

PREPARING FOR WAR

When 2Lt William Henry Brown of No 84 Sqn, Royal Flying Corps (RFC), tilted the nose of his S.E.5a scout earthwards over the Western Front shortly after midday on 14 March 1918, little did he realise that he was setting in motion a train of ideas and events which would circle the globe, via the United States and the Far East, only to return to this very area to wreak havoc some 22 years later.

What made Harry Brown's little fighter so different from the hundreds of other S.E.5as patrolling the skies on that March day was that it had been fitted with a makeshift bomb-rack beneath the fuselage. And the German ammunition barge which he targeted and sank on the canal east of St Quentin that afternoon was fated to become the victim of arguably the world's first deliberate dive-bombing attack.

Despite this initial success, No 84 Sqn did not carry out any further missions of this kind, although a series of carefully controlled tests – using both S.E.5a and Sopwith Camel fighters – were carried out at the RAE Armament Experimental Station at Orfordness on the Suffolk coast in the immediate post-Armistice months. However, the powers-that-be in the Royal Air Force (as the RFC had become on 1 April 1918) decided that any advantages to be gained from precision dive-bombing would be far outweighed by the inevitable heavy losses which could be expected among aircraft and trained pilots engaged in such attacks.

Most of the world's major land-based air forces were of a similar mind. At first, only the United States Naval and Marine Corps air arms championed the dive-bomber concept as offering the best chance of delivering the pinpoint accuracy required to hit small, moving targets at sea.

Meanwhile, in defeated Germany any arguments for or against the dive-bomber as opposed to the traditional high-altitude level bomber were perforce purely academic. Shorn of all offensive weaponry by the 1919 Treaty of Versailles, Germany's arms manufacturers were expressly forbidden from producing any replacements. Hardly was the ink dry on the hated *Diktat*, however, before companies began seeking ways to circumvent the strictures imposed upon them.

One such firm was the Dessau-based Junkers *Flugzeugwerke AG* which, in the early 1920s, set up Swedish subsidiary AB *Flygindustri* at Limhamn-Malmö. Here, they were free to concentrate on military, rather than civil, aircraft production and development. Among the types built at Limhamn was a highly advanced two-seat fighter. Designed by Dipl-Ing Karl Plauth and Hermann Pohlmann, the two Junkers K 47 prototypes, which first flew in 1929, were subsequently evaluated at the clandestine German air

Co-designer of the K 47, Dipl-Ing Hermann Pohlmannn (centre), served with the Imperial German Air Arm in Italy during World War 1. Shot down late in 1917, he became a prisoner of the British. He joined the Junkers company in 1923, and ten years later the then 39-year-old Pohlmann began work on arguably the most famous design of his entire career – the Junkers Ju 87

Equipped with a 480 hp Bristol Jupiter VII engine, the first prototype Junkers K 47 is here seen bearing its initial Swedish civil registration, S-AABW. After subsequent evaluation at Lipezk, this machine – re-engined with the 540 hp Siemens Sh 20 – was assigned to the DVL (German Aviation Experimental Establishment) at Berlin-Adlersdorf as the Junkers A 48 dy, registration D-2012

training centre at Lipezk, north of Voronezh, in the Soviet Union.

And while a batch of 12 production K 47 fighters was completed in Sweden for export (six to the Chinese Cental Government and four ultimately to the Soviet Union), the *Reichswehr* (the 100,000 strong internal army grudgingly allowed Germany by the Versailles signatories) purchased the two prototypes, plus the two remaining export aircraft.

Found to be capable of carrying a 100-kg bomb-load (eight 12.5-kg fragmentation bombs) on their underwing struts, three of these machines were tested at Lipezk for their suitability in the dive-bombing role. Although successful, high unit costs precluded the tightly-budgeted *Reichswehr* from awarding a production contract, and the four aircraft (now designated as A 48s) served out their time in the *Reich* engaged in a variety of quasi-civil duties.

The seed had nevertheless been sown, and in the predatory shape of the original K 47 - despite the uncranked wing and twin tail unit - the embryonic form of the wartime Stuka could already be seen emerging.

A further two aircraft were to play a part in the story of German dive-bomber development before the advent of the Junkers Ju 87, however.

Although the Heinkel He 50 failed miserably as an 'interim dive-bomber', the type was resurrected during the latter half of the war as a night ground-attack aircraft on the Eastern Front. This pair, pictured during the winter of 1943/44, belong to NSGr 11, a unit composed of Estonian volunteers

The first of these came about as a direct result of growing Japanese interest in dive-bombing. Although an erstwhile ally of the Western Powers during World War 1, Japan herself was now also restricted by international treaty in the number, and tonnage, of the capital ships she was permitted to build (a ratio of three-to-two in favour of the United States and Great Britain). Seeking ways to redress the balance, and keenly aware of the ongoing dive-bomber experiments being conducted by the US Navy across the Pacific, Japan turned to Germany for assistance, approaching not Junkers, but the reputable seaplane manufacturing firm of Ernst Heinkel AG.

The resulting two-seater biplane design stressed for diving, and initially equipped with floats, was later exported to Japan as the Heinkel He 50D, and served as the basis for the Imperial Japanese Navy's own Aichi D1A carrier-borne dive-bomber.

Heinkel then offered a second (landplane) prototype to the *Reichswehr*. After a demonstration at the Rechlin test centre in 1932, followed by trials at Lipezk, the type was accepted into service as the He 50A interim dive-bomber in 1933, the year that Adolf Hitler came to power. It was thus the *Reichswehr* under the aegis of the Weimar Republic, and not the new National Socialist regime, which was responsible for preparing the groundwork and introducing the dive-bomber into Germany's covert, but burgeoning, new armoury.

However, Hitler and the head of his still clandestine air force - one Hermann Göring - were more than willing to tread the path already laid down for them. And when World War 1 fighter ace turned international stunt pilot Ernst Udet came back from a tour of the USA in the early 1930s extolling the virtues and dive-bombing abilities of the Curtiss Hawk II fighter then being offered for export, Göring authorised the newly established *Reichsluftfahrtministerium* (German Air Ministry) to provide Udet with the necessary funds to purchase two examples of the type for use in his aerobatic displays. It was a shrewd move, for not only did it give German designers the opportunity to examine state-of-the-art American technology, but also acted as a bribe in tempting the 'freebooting' Udet (who had ended World War 1 in command of Jasta 4 of the *Jagdgeschwader* 'Richthofen' under Göring) back into the official Luftwaffe fold.

The dual-role capability of the Curtiss machines prompted the *Technisches Amt* (Technical Office) of the RLM to issue similar specifications in February 1934 for a single-seat fighter and dive-bomber. The winning design in the shape of the Henschel Hs 123 made its public debut at Berlin-Johannisthal in May of the following year. Flown by Ernst Udet himself, its performance did much to strengthen the hand of the pro-Stuka (i.e. dive-bomber) lobby within the RLM. Yet, if one discounts its early days in Spain, the Henschel was destined never to see action as such. Throughout the whole of its long operational career - it was still flying on the Eastern

Henschel's foray into dive-bomber production in the form of the Hs 123 is now better known for its long, and illustrious, service as a ground-attack aircraft – it too was still active on the Russian Front as late as 1944. This early example, Hs 123A-1 Wk-Nr 858, carries the markings of 3./StG 165, which operated the type between 1936 and 1938

The first prototype Junkers Ju 87 V1 featured a twin-tail unit, but during a medium-angle test dive this assembly began to oscillate. When the pilot attempted to recover, the entire starboard vertical surface parted company with the rest of the tail section, causing the aircraft to crash...

Front in 1944 - the *'eins-zwei-drei'*, or 'one-two-three', was employed to great effect as a low-level close-support aircraft. For despite being the first Stuka design to be ordered in any quantity for the Luftwaffe, the Hs 123 was regarded from the outset as a *'Sofortlösung'* – an 'immediate solution' or temporary measure – to bridge the gap until the second, and final, phase of the dive-bomber programme produced a more advanced two-seater machine offering an improved performance and heavier bomb-load.

To this end, the RLM turned back to Dipl-Ing Hermann Pohlmann of Junkers, co-designer of the original K 47 (Karl Plauth had lost his life in a flying accident before the K 47 was completed). Pohlmann had begun design work on the Ju 87 on his own initiative back in 1933 when the subject of a second phase to the *Sturzbomber-Programm* had first been broached. By the time the official specification was finally issued some two years later, he had already commenced the construction of three prototypes, leaving rival firms Arado and Heinkel well out of the running.

Although obviously a product of the same stable as the K 47, the early Ju 87s were, by contrast, particularly ugly and angular aircraft, characterised by the inverted gull wing which would be the hallmark of every one of the 5700+ Stukas built. But the Ju 87 had been designed to fulfil a specific role, and in this it was unsurpassed, even if (when it was in its natural element swooping almost vertically on its intended target) it was likened somewhat fancifully to an evil bird of prey – 'its radiator bath and fixed, spatted, undercarriage resembled gaping jaws and extended talons'.

...consequently the next two prototypes, the V2 and V3 (pictured), were hastily redesigned with centrally-mounted fin and rudder assemblies

The first prototype Ju 87 V1, powered by a Rolls-Royce Kestrel V 12-cylinder, upright-Vee, liquid-cooled, engine, featured a twin-tail unit not dissimilar to that of its K 47 predecessor. But when this failed in flight during a medium-angle test dive, causing the V1 to crash, the remaining prototypes were redesigned with a centrally-

These two shots of an *'Anton'* and a *'Berta'* – taken from similar angles – clearly illustrate the major external differences between the two. Note the former's smooth upper nose contours, neat rectangular radiator intake, huge trousered and braced undercarriage and hinged-section cockpit canopy with twin aerial mast 'horns'. In contrast, the *'Berta's'* upper cowling is 'stepped' to accommodate the oil cooler intake, whilst the rounded chin radiator is altogether larger and more obtrusive. The new spatted undercarriage may be an aerodynamic improvement, but the same can hardly be said of the sliding-section canopy, with its redesigned rear-gunner's position.

mounted single fin and rudder assembly.

A fourth prototype was later added to the first three, this, the Ju 87 V4, incorporating all the lessons learned from flight-testing the original trio. With its Junkers Jumo 210Aa inverted-Vee engine in a revised, lowered, cowling to improve forward visibility, re-contoured cockpit canopy and enlarged vertical tail surfaces, the V4 led directly to the first batch of fully-armed Ju 87A-0 pre-production models which started coming off the assembly line before the end of 1936. These in turn were followed during the course of 1937 by the A-1 and A-2 production runs, the latter being equipped with the uprated Jumo 210Da engine.

In 1938, hard on the heels of the last *'Anton'* to be built, there appeared the first of the *'Bertas'*. When compared to the Ju 87A, the B-model featured not just a more powerful Jumo 211 engine with direct fuel injection, but a completely redesigned and reconstructed fuselage, cockpit and vertical tail. The most striking difference between the two, however, was the abandonment of the *'Anton's'* huge 'trousered' undercarriage in favour of the slightly less obtrusive, and therefore aerodynamically cleaner, spatted leg.

By the outbreak of World War 2, the Ju 87A had already been withdrawn from first-line service and relegated to training units. On the opening morning of hostilities the Luftwaffe's operational Stuka force, composed almost entirely of early Ju 87Bs, numbered exactly 346, of which all but 22 were serviceable.

This *'Anton'* of *Stuka Vorschule* 1 (Dive Bomber Preliminary School 1) was still in service as a trainer at Bad Aibling in the winter of 1940-41. *'Irene'* was the girlfriend of pilot-instructor August Diemer. Note that the lower sections of the undercarriage trousers have been removed to prevent a build-up of compacted snow

CONDOR LEGION

On the night of 1 August 1936 the steamship *Usaramo* slipped quietly out of Hamburg harbour. At first light some five days later she docked at Cadiz, in southern Spain, and began discharging her cargo. This included six crated He 51s, twenty 20 mm anti-aircraft pieces, some 100 tons of additional war material and 86 thinly-disguised civil 'tourists'. Although subjected to several salvoes from an offshore Spanish Republican destroyer, all was landed safely. The *Usaramo* had been carrying as 'cargo' some of the first participants of *Unternehmen 'Zauberfeuer'* (Operation *Magic Fire*), Hitler's response to the appeal for help from Gen Franco, head of the Nationalist coup against the Spanish Government which had been launched from Spanish Morocco less than three weeks earlier. After landing, the men and supplies were immediately ferried to Nationalist-held Seville, meeting up at the town's Tablada airfield with ten Ju 52 transports flown in directly from Germany by captains and crews of the state airline Lufthansa. The build-up of the *Condor Legion* had begun.

As part of a later shipment in November, the contents of one crate also convoyed to Tablada for assembly was surrounded by the utmost secrecy. This was a single machine plucked from the pre-production batch of Ju 87A-0s freshly rolled off the Dessau assembly line. Allocated the military serial 29-1 and piloted by Unteroffizier Hermann Beuer, it was assigned to VJ/88, the experimental *Staffel* of the *Legion*'s fighter wing which comprised not only three prototype Bf 109s and a cannon-armed prototype of the He 112, but also three Hs 123s which had arrived some weeks earlier.

Little is known of 29-1's subsequent career in Spain, other than that it transferred with VJ/88 from Tablada up to Vitoria, in northern Castile, in February 1937 to take part in the Nationalist offensive against Bilbao. It was reportedly still at Vitoria some five months later but, shrouded in secrecy to the end, is presumed to have been shipped back to the *Reich* from one of the newly-captured Spanish Biscay ports shortly thereafter.

In mid-January 1938 three Ju 87A-1s arrived at Vitoria, these machines hailing from IV.(St)/LG 1's 11.*Staffel* based at Barth. Now coded 29-2, -3 and -4 (and initially piloted by Unteroffizier Ernst Bartels and Oberleutnante Gerhard Weyert and Hermann Haas respectively), they were officially incorporated into the *Legion* as the fighter wing's fifth *Staffel* (5.J/88), but became universally known as the 'Jolanthe' *Kette* after their unit badge. This depicted a large pink sow, and could trace its origins back to Barth, where the *Gruppenkommandeur* of IV.(St)/LG 1, Oberstleutnant Günther Schwartzkopff

The first real test came in Spain. Previous assertions that the machine illustrated here is '29.1' – the single Ju 87A-0 sent to Spain in November 1936 – would seem to be disproved by the presence of another Ju 87 alongside it ('29.1' was reportedly returned to the Reich several months before the arrival of the 'Jolanthe' *Kette* in mid-January 1938). It would point too to the latter's using another badge, described by one source as an 'umbrella superimposed on a derby hat' (a tongue-in-cheek reference to their 'civilian' status while en route to Spain), before they adopted the famous pink pig

And here is 'Jolanthe' in all her glory on the port undercarriage trouser of a bombed-up *'Anton'*. But this machine poses another puzzle as all references are adamant that only three Ju 87A-1s served with the *Condor Legion*, yet this *'Anton'* clearly displays the individual number '5'! Was a fourth aircraft sent to replace a hitherto unrecorded loss among the original trio, were the *Kette's* numbers altered at intervals to confuse the enemy, or is this simply a machine painted up for propaganda purposes?

(one of the most fervent supporters of the Stuka concept) had nicknamed the Ju 87 after the eponymous heroine of a favourite film comedy of the day that centred around a pig – *'Krach um Jolanthe'* ('Trouble with Iolanthe')!

On 7 February the *Kette* moved up to Calamocha, this barren sandy field south of Zaragoza serving as J/88's major base during the battle of Teruel. And it was here that the Ju 87s began to put into operational practice what up till now had only been theory. One of the first things they discovered was that the *'Anton's'* trousered undercarriage did not like Calamocha's soft surface, and that take-offs and landings were much easier if the wheel fairings were removed – a portent of Russian spring mud four years hence! It was also found that the Ju 87A's 500-kg bomb-load could only be carried if the rear cockpit seat was empty. The normal offensive load in Spain therefore had to be restricted to a 250-kg bomb.

During the latter half of March the *Kette* undertook a number of precision dive-bombing attacks on bridges and other targets as Republican forces retreated across Aragon – not always with the desired results, it must be admitted. In these early days near misses nearly always outnumbered direct hits by a substantial margin, but they were learning their trade nonetheless. And as new crews from the homeland replaced the original trio on a rotational basis, a steady stream of returnees to the *Reich* were taking back with them an invaluable pool of practical experience.

Transferring forward to La Cenia, the *'Antons'* supported both the advance on Valencia and the subsequent breakthrough to the Mediterranean coast. Following this run of Nationalist successes, they proved their worth during the Republican counter-offensive along the Ebro late in July. On the 27th alone, the trio mounted four separate attacks on enemy troop concentrations and crossing points south of Mequinenza. With the Republicans finally broken once and for all, the way was left open for the final push through Catalonia to the French border. But the

A massed take-off by the *Legion's* entire Stuka arm! All three A-1s of the 'Jolanthe' *Kette* kick up dust as they gather speed across Calamocha's sandy surface

With full bomb loads, a *Kette* of 'Bertas' head for a Republican target. Another shot for the markings 'buffs', this photo shows the leader's aircraft wearing the codes '29.11'. This would seem to indicate that the five B-1s sent to Spain were not numbered sequentially with the four (or five?) original 'Antons'

'Iolanthe' *Kette* did not witness the end, for after several attacks on shipping in Tarragona and other Mediterranean ports, the three war-weary *'Antons'* were quietly returned to Germany in October 1938.

They were replaced in Spain by five Ju 87B-1s, but so effective had their predecessors been that the newcomers found little to do. Capable of carrying a full 500-kg bomb-load, they were attached, more fittingly, to 5.K/88 – the fifth *Staffel* of the *Legion's* bomber wing. During the closing weeks of the Catalonian offensive they sometimes accompanied larger formations of He 111s attacking enemy positions. The *'Bertas'* also saw limited action on the Madrid front in mid-March 1939, but were no longer present to participate in the great victory display that was staged some two months later. Crated up, they were spirited out of Spain as quietly and unobtrusively as the single Ju 87A-0 had been smuggled in some 30 months earlier.

The experience gained from the handful of Stukas sent to participate in the Spanish Civil War was indeed invaluable. Air and groundcrews alike practised and perfected their skills and techniques, equipment was honed and numerous modifications made. But one ingredient had been lacking – serious opposition. In the air the Ju 87s enjoyed strong fighter protection, whilst effective Republican anti-aircraft fire was almost non-existent except in the immediate vicinity of those targets deemed to be vitally important.

A great feeling of confidence in the dive-bomber had therefore been engendered by the Stuka's performance in Spain. No bad thing, and one which would serve the crews well in the opening months of the war that was to come. However, in one important respect the Ju 87 remained untested – its ability to survive in a completely hostile airspace.

Although no Ju 87s were lost in Spain, not all returned unscathed. This exit hole in the port tailplane of an unidentified *'Berta'* is evidence of the unwelcome attentions of Republican anti-aircraft gunners

THE *BLITZKRIEG* ERA: POLAND

It was no accident that the Ju 87 was selected to carry out the very first operation of World War 2, which was initiated some 20 minutes before the official outbreak of hostilities! Given the nature of the objective, no other choice was possible .

The easternmost province of the *Reich*, East Prussia, was cut off from Germany proper by the Polish Corridor. This hotly disputed strip of territory, which afforded the landlocked Poles access to the Baltic Sea, was another product of the Treaty of Versailles, and a contributory factor in Hitler's decision to attack Poland. Across its neck ran a single railway which connected the province to Berlin. This track would be a vital lifeline between the two in time of war. Its weakest link was the bridge at Dirschau (Tczew), where it spanned the River Vistula. Both Germans and Poles were aware of this, and the latter had prepared the bridge for demolition should they be attacked.

The target for the first bombing raid of the war was therefore not the bridge itself, but the demolition ignition points situated in blockhouses at nearby Dirschau station, plus the cables which ran out along the railway embankment on to the bridge. The objective was to prevent the structure from being destroyed before it could be seized by German ground troops being transported into Poland by armoured train. It was a job that only the Stuka could do.

Wearing civilian clothes, pilots of I./StG 1 – the unit ordered to carry out the attack – had undertaken their own first-hand reconnaissance by travelling back and forth several times in the sealed trains (inevitably known as 'corridor trains') in which Germans were allowed to traverse the 100-km stretch of line that connected East Prussia with the Fatherland.

Ju 87B-1 'A5+DH' of I./StG 1, the *Gruppe* which carried out the first bombing raid of World War 2 . . .

At exactly 04.26 hours on 1 September 1939 a *Kette* of Ju 87s of 3./StG 1, led by *Staffelkapitän* Oberleutnant Bruno Dilley, lifted off from their forward base in East Prussia for the eight-minute flight to the target. Despite the all-pervading ground-mist which blanketed the area, the trio of Stukas, each loaded with one 250-kg bomb, plus four smaller 50-kg weapons slung in

. . . and the target of that mission, the railway station at Dirschau (Tczew) in the Polish Corridor. Note one of the blockhouses in the left foreground which protected the ignition points for the demolition cables running out to the bridge (just visible in the background to the right of the ruined station building) carrying the railway over the River Vistula

The wrecked spans of the bridge which were destroyed by Polish army engineers before the arrival of German troops. Both this and the preceding photograph were taken after the area was finally occupied

pairs under each wing, soon spotted the unmistakable iron lattice-work of the bridge looming ahead of them. Flying at a height of just ten metres above the flat Vistula plain, the three pilots climbed as one before separating to plant their bombs unerringly on the station blockhouses, severing the finger-thick cables. Despite successfully completing their mission, it was all to no avail. The armoured train was delayed, and the Poles managed to destroy the bridge before German ground troops could reach it.

The first bombing raid of the war had been a carefully planned – albeit ultimately abortive – operation. That the Ju 87 could also lay claim to the first aerial victory of World War 2 came about quite by chance.

Elements of I./StG 2 'Immelmann' from Nieder-Ellguth in Upper Silesia had taken part in an early morning mixed-formation bombing raid on the Polish airfield at Krakow, but they had arrived at their target to

An impressive line-up of Ju 87B-2s of I./StG 2 'Immelmann' each bearing the *Gruppe's* distinctive Scottie-dog emblem, in the case of 1.*Staffel* - as here - on a white disc

find it deserted – most Polish Air Force units vacated their peacetime bases and dispersed to prearranged, carefully concealed, satellite fields in the hours leading up to the invasion. Whilst returning from Krakow after dropping their ordnance on empty hangars, a gaggle of Stukas happened to overfly one such field near the village of Balice just as a pair of PZL P.11c fighters of No 121 Sqn were scrambling. Still clawing for altitude, but already intent on destroying one of the Ju 87s up ahead, the leader of the pair, Capt Mieczyslaw Medwecki (the CO of No 121), failed to spot another trio of Stukas closing up behind him. It took barely a few seconds for *Kettenführer* Leutnant Frank Neubert to overhaul the unwitting Polish pilot and then line up his wing guns. His aim was good, for his burst of fire hit the fighter's cockpit and caused Medwecki's PZL to 'suddenly explode in mid-air, bursting apart like a huge fireball – the fragments literally flew around our ears'.

As well as attempting to wipe out the Polish Air Force on the ground, Luftwaffe planners also targeted the small, but modern, Polish Navy. Not surprisingly, the naval 4.(St)/TrGr 186 was heavily involved in these attacks. The widespread mist over the coastal regions on the opening morning of the war thwarted the *Staffel's* first planned raid on Westerplatte, but conditions had improved enough by the afternoon for a second mission to be mounted against Hela. Approaching at 7000 metres,

A heavy ground mist covered much of the Baltic coastal provinces during the early hours of the opening morning of hostilities. Here, fully armed machines of the *Geschwaderstab* StG 2 'Immelmann' ('T6+CA' foreground) still await the first mission of the day among bombs already placed in position for their return and rearming for a second sortie

Crewmen inspect flak damage to the tailplane and rear fuselage of an unidentified *'Berta'* after a mission over Poland

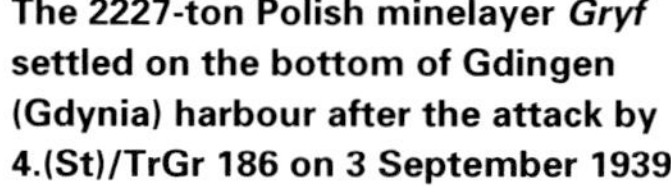

The 2227-ton Polish minelayer *Gryf* settled on the bottom of Gdingen (Gdynia) harbour after the attack by 4.(St)/TrGr 186 on 3 September 1939

the four *Ketten* winged over into their dive. However, unlike targets in Spain, or the bridge over the River Vistula, the tiny harbour and naval strongpoint at Hela (situated at the very tip of the long, slender, peninsula of the same name) was defended by one of the biggest anti-aircraft batteries in all of Poland. Bracketed by fire as they plummeted from 5500 down to 700 metres, the Stukas lost two of their number in this, their very first engagement. In fact Hela, although under constant attack from land, sea and air, would resist until the very end. Its beleaguered defenders did not surrender until 1 October, some four days after Warsaw had fallen. Subsequent German investigations revealed that 4.(St)/TrGr 186's initial attack must have been launched in the face of some 250 individual anti-aircraft barrels!

On 3 September the *Staffel* hit the main Polish naval base at Gdingen (Gdynia), where they sank the 1540-ton destroyer *Wicher* and badly damaged the minelayer *Gryf.* However, despite destroying numerous other coastal targets, time and again the unit returned to Hela. *Staffelkapitän* Hauptmann Blattner, an ex-transatlantic captain with Lufthansa, described one such raid:

'Three minutes after the orders for the attack were received we were in the air. We climbed away from our base (Stolp-West, on the German side of the Corridor) and had reached our normal operating height of 7000

The famous 'doctored' photo of a machine of 4.(St)/TrGr 186 returning from a raid on Hela with its undercarriage legs 'sheared off' after accidentally hitting the water . . .

metres by the time we crossed the coast at Rixhöft. I led the *Staffel* in a wide arc out to sea, intending to approach the tip of Hela out of the sun from the east.

'I could see little through the broken cloud below, but over on our right another *Gruppe* (IV.(St)/LG 1) on its way to Gdingen was catching heavy flak. Then it was our turn. My observer called out the positions of the shell bursts, some 100 to 150 metres away from us, as we neared the objective.

'All thoughts of the flak were driven from my mind as I led the *Staffel* down in a steep dive. Despite the apparent confusion, each aircraft was aiming at a pre-assigned target. Our weeks of training against the old *Hessen* (a 13,000-ton turn of the century battleship, rebuilt as a radio-controlled target ship in 1936-37) had not been wasted!'

It was also while attacking Hela that another of the Staffel's Ju 87C-0s was severely damaged by anti-aircraft fire. Its pilot actuated the explosive bolts which jettisoned the main undercarriage preparatory to ditching at sea. In the event, he managed to stagger back to base where he carried out a successful belly landing. The German propaganda machine seized upon this incident to extol the strength and structural integrity of the Stuka, claiming the undercarriage had been wiped off when the machine accidentally hit the water while pulling out of a dive. They even distributed a photograph purportedly showing the stricken machine during its return flight. The photo was a complete fake.

Having helped disable - or, to a greater or lesser extent, neutralise - Poland's air and sea forces in the opening hours of the invasion, the *Stukagruppen* were now freed to embark upon their main tactical role of 'flying artillery', clearing a path ahead, and to the flanks, of the advancing German Panzers and ground columns. The lightning war tactics of co-ordinated fire, support and rapid advance – the 'Blitzkrieg' – was about to be unleashed upon an unsuspecting Europe still immured in World War 1 traditions and practices.

In mid-afternoon of 1 September it was the turn of StG 77. For some of this unit's pilots it was already their fourth mission of the day (the first, scheduled at 04.45 hours, had been flown against Polish border

. . . and the original shot used to create the fake, which in fact portrays a brace of *'Bertas'* of the *Condor Legion* over Spain!

Once the fog had lifted the *Stukagruppen* were on constant call to assist the advancing ground troops. Here, a unit waits in the September sun for its next mission, bombs having already been placed on the ground in readiness below the wings of the nearest aircraft – the risk of retaliatory strikes by the Polish Air Force was obviously not regarded as being very great!

Each machine carrying a single 500-kg bomb, a *Kette* lifts off from a forward field en route to a Polish target

Ju 87Bs echeloned to starboard, ready to peel off into a line-astern attack

Once over the target area each aircraft selected, or was assigned, a specific objective. This well-known photograph of a *'Berta'* unleashing a full load of single 250-kg bomb, plus four underwing 50-kg bombs, was also the subject of some propaganda skullduggery . . .

. . . for when placed against a different cloud formation, with an industrial landscape added below, another 'enemy' target can be shown to be facing certain destruction!

fortifications near Lublinitz). The *Gruppe* logbook recorded, 'In complete contrast to the early morning, when we had quite literally taken off blind into the mist, the field was now bathed in sunshine. Not a cloud in the clear blue sky'.

All 60 Ju 87s of I. and II./StG 77 were ordered to concentrate their attack on the same large farm complex north of Wielun which, it had now been confirmed, housed the headquarters of the Polish *Wolynska* cavalry brigade. It was annihilated, the troops scattered, and Wielun was occupied by the advancing Germans that same night.

Thus, on the very first afternoon of hostilities, the pattern had been set for the remainder of the brief campaign as Stukas and Panzers combined to smash through Poland's frontier defences (at the same time, incidentally, providing the world with an enduring image of Polish cavalry gallantly charging enemy tanks). For as the 24 infantry divisions and six mounted brigades of Poland's western armies were pushed inexorably back – the majority of them retiring towards the capital, Warsaw – the Ju 87s kept up their continual harassment.

No sooner did one of the 350+ reconnaissance machines (which played such a vital role in the *Wehrmacht's* success in Poland) radio back a report,

A daunting sight as serried ranks of Ju 87s wing towards their objective

Poland's rail network suffered heavily at the hands of the Stukas as the Luftwaffe sought to disrupt the enemy's lines of communication and supply. Targets included armoured trains, this one having been derailed by a near miss on the neighbouring track

than a formation of Stukas would immediately be despatched to the trouble spot, be it a particularly stubborn defence position, a large body of enemy troops, a road or rail line or a bridge offering a route of escape for the retreating Poles.

As the German spearheads bit into Poland, so the close-support *Stukagruppen* had to move forward too in order to keep pace with them. Sometimes they ran the risk of over-reaching themselves. Oskar Dinort, *Gruppenkommandeur* of I.StG 2 recalls:

'We moved up into Poland. Our new base was some seven kilometres outside the town of Tschenstochau (Czestochowa). We arrived about midday and the base personnel immediately set about erecting tents and organising defensive positions. We were, after all, on enemy soil and the woods bordering the field to the north-east were reportedly full of Polish stragglers . . .

'. . . sure enough, hardly had darkness fallen before shots rang out from the edge of the woods. Our ground-staff replied with machine-guns and light flak. The whole field was eerily illuminated by flickering searchlight beams and red beads of tracer. The firing continued throughout the night, but died out shortly after 4 am when it started to rain. At last we aircrew could snatch some sleep.'

Dinort and his crews got all the rest they needed. The rain persisted,

A pair of Ju 87B-Is of Major Dinort's I./St G 2 'Immelmann', each armed with a single SC 250 (250-kg general-purpose) bomb, set out on another mission

and they did not take off until 3 pm the next afternoon. Their targets were the bridges over the Vistula near the fort of Modlin, to the north of Warsaw;

Poland's rivers were a great aid to navigation in an otherwise often featureless landscape. A loosely-formatted *Kette* overflies one such waterway, clearly delineated by the evening sun, as it makes its way back to base

'We climbed through the grey clouds and broke out into clearer air at some 1200 metres. Below us the ragged valleys of cumuli, above us a leaden, sunless sky.

'Course north-east. Visibility was still not good. The windscreen streaked with more rain. Only the occasional glimpse of the ground and brief sighting of the Vistula through a break in the clouds to keep us on track. At last I saw the fort below us. It lay in the brown landscape, huge, grey and pointed like some burned-out star. And there too the Vistula bridges. Tiny lighter strips against the dark bed of the river: our target.

'The moment has come. Wing over into the dive! The machine drops like a stone. The altitude unwinds – down 200 metres, 300, 500. The instruments can hardly keep pace with the rate of descent. Then the red veil in front of the eyes that every Stuka pilots knows. 1400 metres from the ground. . . 1200 metres . . . press the release. The bomb falls away into the depths below.

'I recover and take the usual evasive measures. Jinking away, I look back. Behind me the *Stabskette* are in the middle of their dive, the first *Staffel* right on their tails, dark shadows against the lightening sky. Their aim is good . . . one bomb hits the centre of the target.'

As the Polish retreat gathered pace and increasing numbers of their army units became compressed into ever smaller areas, dangerous pockets of potential resistance were created. South of Radom some six Polish divisions became thus entrapped while pulling back towards the safety of the Vistula. The encircling Panzers called up the Stukas to force them into surrender, Oberst Günter Schwartzkopff's I. and II./StG 77, reinforced

While the 8./StG 2 groundcrew, their work done, choose either to relax in the sun or seek the shade of a Stuka's wing, it is the SC 250 bomb in the foreground which here provides a wealth of detail for the modeller. Lying on its side, with its top towards the cameraman, it proves to be a two-fuse model, the two metallic fuse heads being clearly visible. The left-hand stencil ('15' in a circle) indicates a Type 15 electrical impact fuse, the middle stencil 'B' identifies the particular version of the bomb (one of eight), and the '14' refers to the type of explosive contained in the warhead. Note too the suspension eye bolt on the steel band and the lug seen here projecting upwards. The latter was one of two positioned on either side of the bomb and designed to engage the fork mechanism of the ventral cradle which swung the bomb clear of the propeller when it was released in the dive. The whole was normally finished in green-grey paint.

by III./StG 51 and I./StG 76 (over 150 aircraft in all), pounding the hapless Poles. After enduring four days of near-constant attack, the banshee wail of diving Stukas dropping their deadly 50-kg fragmentation bombs and then ground-strafing with machine-guns, the demoralised survivors gave up.

An even greater danger threatened some days later. Completely surrounded west of Warsaw, the Polish *Poznan* Army – still practically intact – struck south-eastwards across the River Bzura, also aiming to reach the Vistula. This attempt to break through the thin screen of the German 8.*Armee* on the far bank of the Bzura would, if successful, completely cut off the forward most 10.*Armee*, which was already probing into the suburbs of Warsaw. *Heeresgruppe Süd* (Army Group South) sent out urgent appeals to the Luftwaffe for a 'maximum effort' against the Kutno area (the centre of the 80-km wide Polish pocket).

In the ensuing 'Battle of Bzura Cauldron' – an essentially air-versus-ground engagement which finally broke the back of organised Polish resistance – the Stukas played a major role.

And so it went on until the last surviving remnants of the *Poznan* Army laid down their arms. With the danger to its rear eliminated, the *Wehrmacht* prepared for the final assault on Warsaw. The Luftwaffe, too, resumed its interrupted bombing campaign against the Polish capital. Initially, the *Stukagruppen* had been employed against specific pinpoint targets. These were often strongly defended and inevitably led to damage and losses among the attackers.

Despite inflicting much damage on Luftwaffe aircraft during the numerous raids on Warsaw, the city's anti-aircraft defences were eventu-

As the Blitzfrieg drew to a close, formations of Stukas roared unchallenged and unopposed low over the flat plains of central Poland

ally overwhelmed. By this stage most of the twin-engined bomber units had already been withdrawn to the west, leaving the final raids on the battered capital to be performed by Stukas dropping high-explosive bombs in level flight, followed by lumbering three-engined Ju 52s whose crews shovelled out incendiaries just to add to the carnage on the ground.

After Warsaw fell on 27 September there remained only the Modlin forts, some 25 kilometres to the north-west of the capital, to be subjugated. For the last time in Poland the Stukas gathered – units such as IV.(St)/LG 1, which had been exclusively briefed to pound the Baltic coastal defences, were brought in to add their weight to the attack. The Modlin defenders suffered several days of aerial onslaught before eventually surrendering to troops from the SS Regiment *Deutschland* on 29 September.

Forty-eight hours later Hela hoisted the white flag and it was all over. Poland had been overrun and a new word – *'Blitzkrieg'* – had entered the world's vocabulary. It had all cost the *Stukawaffe* just 31 Ju 87s.

The winter of 1939-40 was a time of rest and recuperation in the Homeland for the ***Stukagruppen***. Few had it quite as cushy as the men of III./StG 2, however, their base at Ollesheim outside Düren, being situated right alongside the local suburban tramline – a service much in demand at the end of the day's work!

Ju 87B-1 '35+G12' of 2./StG 163 'Immelmann', Cottbus, February 1939

A standard finished 'Berta' wearing the five-part military designation first introduced on 1 June 1936. The two digits to the left of the fuselage cross indicate, respectively, the *Luftkreis-kommando* (local air command) (3) and the numerical sequence of the Geschwader within that *Luftkreis* (5). To the right of the cross is the aircraft's individual identity code letter (G). This is followed by the *Gruppe* (1) and the *Staffel* (2) digits. Unusually, 2./StG 163 Ju 87s at this time also carried non-military style individual numbers on their cowlings.

Ju 87A-1 '35+Y25' of 5./StG 163 'Immelmann', Grottkau/Silesia, January 1939

StG 163's 'Antons' wore the standard early three-colour upper surface camouflage of dark-brown, green and grey, with light-blue undersides. As part of the second *Staffel* within its particular *Gruppe* (II. *Gruppen* normally consisted of 4., 5. and 6. *Staffeln*), the individual aircraft letter is again red as above. The overpainting of the red band behind the tail swastika puts the date as post-1 January 1939.

Ju 87A-1 '52+A12' of 2./StG 165, Pocking, March 1938

Depicted at the time of the annexation of Austria, this machine wears a similar three-tone camouflage to that above, albeit with the colours transposed. The red tail band with the swastika on a white disc was the standard tail marking for all military aircraft between 15 September 1935 and 1 January 1939.

Ju 87B-2 'J9+IH' of 7./StG 1, Ostende/ Belgium, January 1941

III./StG 1 had previously been I.(St)/TrGr 186, and this Gruppe too retained its previous unit codes long after its redesignation in July 1940. The temporary black undersides and overpainting of all white markings and insignia point to 'Ida-Heinrich's' participation in the nocturnal attacks on south-east England early in 1941. Many aircraft of this Gruppe also carried the names of previous actions on their engine cowlings including 'Boulogne' and 'Lee-on-Solent'.

Ju 87A-1 '29.2' of 5.J/88 *Condor Legion,* Vitoria/Spain, January 1938

One of the original trio of A-1s sent to Spain at the beginning of 1938, '29.2' displays standard three-tone Luftwaffe camouflage with Nationalist Spanish insignia applied: a solid black fuselage disc, a diagonal black cross on the white rudder and reversed wing markings of a white cross on a black disc. Note too the white wingtips.

Ju 87A-1 '29.4' of 5.J/88 *Condor Legion* Calamocha/Spain, February 1938

29.4 was the mount of Leutnant Hermann Haas – the first *Kettenführer* of 5.J/88 – and his wireless-operator/gunner, Feldwebel Emil Kramer. Now unofficially, but universally, known as the 'Jolanthe-Kette', 29.4 sports the famous pink pig badge on its undercarriage trousers, the lower fairings of which have been re-moved to improve take-off and landing runs across Calamocha's soft and sandy surface.

Ju 87B-1 '29.6' of 5.J/88 *Condor Legion,* Catalonia/Spain, January 1939

'Antons' were replaced by 'Bertas' late in 1938. The newcomers also combined standard Luftwaffe camouflage – now the new two-tone green – with Nationalist Spanish markings as depicted here. Although attached to the *'Legion's* bomber wing, several of the 'Bertas' continued to wear the original *'Jolanthe-Kette'* emblem on their wheelspats.

Ju 87B-1 '6G+LT' of 6./StG 1, Norrent-Fontès/France, August 1940

When StG 1 was brought up to full *Geschwader* status in July 1940 the second *Gruppe* slot was filled by redesignating the erstwhile III./StG 51. For some time II./StG 1 retained both their old *Gruppe* badge (a torch-bearing devil astride a bomb) and their previous fuselage codes, as witness 'Ludwig-Theodor' here – an ex-9./StG 51 machine.

Ju 87A-1 "81+E11" del 1./StG 168, Graz-Thalerhof, April 1938

After its incorporation into the Greater German Reich, Austria became officially known as the *'Ostmark'*. The only *Stukagruppe* based in the newly-annexed 'Eastern border region' was I./StG 168, represented here by 'E-Emil'.

Ju 87B-1 'T6+CA' of *Stab* StG 2 'Immelmann', Cologne-Ostheim, May 1940

A standard finish B-1 of the *Geschwaderstab* StG 2 'Immelmann' in French campaign markings, complete with new enlarged underwing crosses. Note the small propellers on the undercarriage leg fairings. These were intended to add an extra dimension of terror by emitting an unearthly howl during the dive, but were soon removed by most units because of their adverse effect on the Stuka's already marginal performance in level flight.

Ju 87B-2 'T6+KH' of 1./StG 2 'Immelmann', Cologne-Ostheim, May 1940

All I./StG 2 aircraft were initially distinguished by their prominent *Gruppe* badge. Modelled on Major Hitschhold's pet scottie 'Molch', this was carried on a disc in the respective *Staffel* colours – white for 1./StG 2.

Ju 87B-2 'T6+HL' of 3./StG 2 'Immelmann', St Malo/France, August 1940

Otherwise identical to 1.*Staffel's* 'Kurfürst-Heinrich', this machine wears the yellow trim and the code letter 'L' of 3./StG 2. Note too that although retaining the yellow disc (which presumably once carried the *Gruppe's* scottie-dog emblem), 3.*Staffel* opted instead for the coat-of-arms of the city of Breslau, their home station back in 1937.

Ju 87B-2 'T6+GM' of 4./StG 2 'Immelmann', Siegburg, May 1940

Unlike I.*Gruppe*, the component Staffeln of II./StG 2 each had their own individual badge from the outset, that of 4.*Staffel* being the lucky four-leaf clover depicted here. This machine also combines a new-style fuselage cross with pre-1940 positioned tail swastika. Note the small 'screamers' attached to the fins of the underwing bombs. The Luftwaffe christened these screamers *'Jericho-Trompeten'* – 'Trumpets of Jericho'!

Ju 87B-2 'T6+KN' of 5./StG 2 'Immelmann', Lannion/France, August 1940

A regulation set of markings – swastika correctly located on the tailfin – for 5.*Staffel's* 'Kurfürst-Nordpol', together with the unit's 'aggressive penguin' badge below the windscreen and the individual aircraft letter 'K' in black, thinly outlined in red.

Ju 87B-1 'T6+RT' of 9./StG 2 'Immelmann', Nörvenich, May 1940

III./StG 2's *Staffeln* also favoured individual emblems. Here, the 'dancing devil' on the yellow shield, plus the yellow spinner tip and individual aircraft letter, carried in conjunction with the *Staffel* code letter 'T', all point conclusively to 9./StG 2.

Ju 87B-1 'S7+NL' of 3./StG 3, Caen/France, August 1940

The only *Stukagruppe* to have been stationed in pre-war Austria, I./StG 76 must have retained a certain sense of isolation even after its redesignation as I./StG 3 immediately prior to the Battle of Britain, for the other two *Gruppen* of the embryonic StG 3 were not created until 1942! Known as the 'Graz *Gruppe*' since its earliest days as I./StG 168, this unit also selected the coat-of-arms of its home town as its identifying badge.

Ju 87B-2 '6G+CD' of *Stab* III./StG 51, Cologne-Wahn, May 1940

Another example of new-style fuselage cross combined with a tail swastika overlapping both fin and rudder, 'Cäsar-Dora' also illustrates this *Geschwaderstab*'s unusual presentation of its unit codes – variously described as pale grey or (more likely) light green – during the campaign in France. The *Gruppenstab* badge is another geographical reference, depicting the 'Eagle of Tyrol'.

Ju 87B-1 '6G+FR' of 7./StG 51, France, June 1940

Perhaps the most flamboyant of all Stuka unit emblems of the early war years, 7./StG 51's badge combined a charging bull on a yellow star background beneath the windscreen, with a yellow comet tail stretching back almost the entire length of the cockpit canopy.

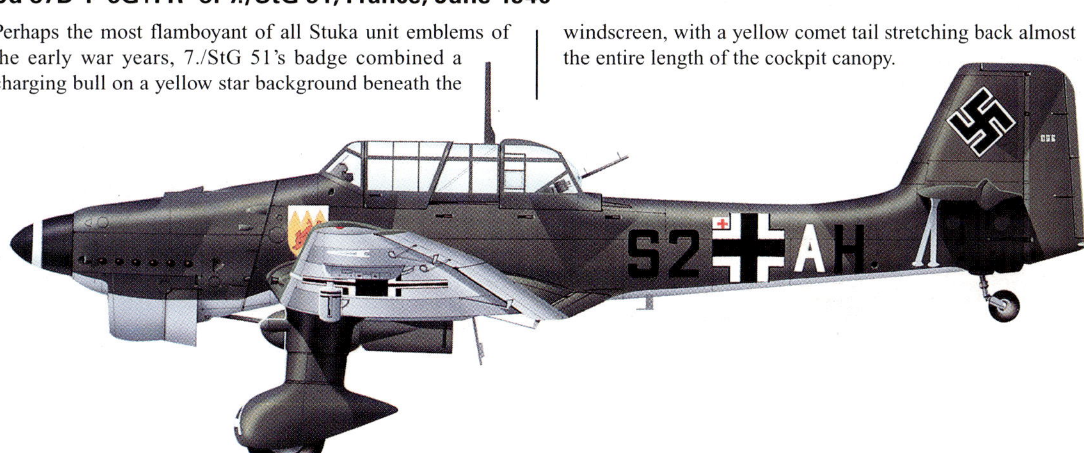

Ju 87B-1 'S2+AH' of 1./StG 77, Caen-Maltot/France, August 1940

StG 77 had arguably the most regimented system of unit badges of any Ju 87 *Gruppe*. Every aircraft in the *Geschwader* bore the same yellow shield with an indented upper field in the respective *Stab* or *Gruppe* colour. Each unit, from *Geschwaderstab* down-wards, also had its own device on the main body of the shield – in the case of I.*Staffel* this was a leaping pig. The individual aircraft letter 'A' identifies this as the machine of the *Staffelkapitän*, Oberleutnant Trogemann.

Ju 87B-1 'S2+EM' of 4./StG 77, Cologne-Butzweilerhof, May 1940

Conforming to *Geschwader* regulations, this otherwise perfectly standard B-1 features the unit badge with a red upper segment indicating II.*Gruppe* and *Staffel* emblem of a crowing cockerel. Note that the fairing for the propeller siren on 'Emil-Martha's' undercarriage leg has been capped off by a flat plate.

Ju 87A-2 'S13+S29' of an unidentified training unit, Nuremberg area, circa early 1939

Although superficially similar to operational unit codes of the pre-war period, the fuselage markings on trainers did differ. To the left of the fuselage cross, the first 'S' stood for *Schule* (school), the following digit(s) indicating the school's territorial command area (in this instance *Luftgaukommando* XIII Nürnberg). The letter to the right of the cross (confusingly in this case another 'S') identified the training flight within the school, and it was the closing digit(s) – here 'White 29' – which provided the aircraft's individual identity.

Ju 87B-2 'F1+AC' of *Stab* III./StG 77, Caen/France, August 1940

Unable to use yellow for the upper segment of their badges, III./StG 77 elected for blue instead. The *Gruppenstab* emblem on the main yellow field was a knight on horseback, the family crest of the *Kommandeur* Hauptmann Helmuth Bode – certain members of the *Stab* unkindly suggested that the insignia on the knight's shield, three yellow stars and a yellow disc, stood for three-star brandy and a glass of beer viewed from above!

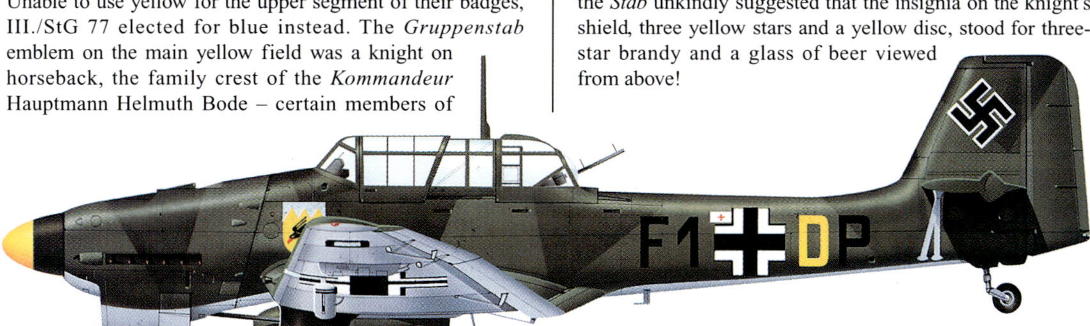

Ju 87B-2 'F1+DP' of 9./StG 77, Caen/France, August 1940

Very similar overall to Bode's Stuka, the aircraft of 9.*Staffel* featured a far less imaginative badge. They selected as their emblem a diving eagle clutching a bomb in its talons. Note, however, that all Ju 87s of III./StG 77, including both 'Anton-Cäsar' and 'Dora-Paula', initially retained the fuselage codes of the unit from which they were formed – the Do 17-equipped II./KG 76.

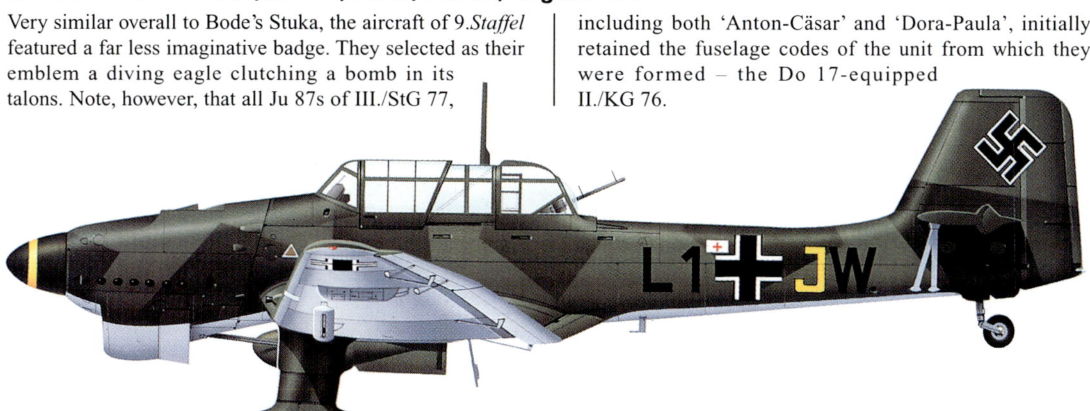

Ju 87B-1 'L1+JW' of 12.(St)/LG 1, Stolp-Reitz, September 1939

Wearing standard markings for the early months of the war (thin-edged fuselage cross and tail swastika on the rudder hinge line), this B-1 is identifiable solely by its fuselage code, IV.(St)/LG 1's *Gruppe* badge not yet having been applied.

Ju 87B-1 'J9+TM' of 4.(St)/TrGr 186, Stolp-West, September 1939

Operating as a single *Staffel* during the Polish campaign, the aircraft of 4.(St)/TrGr 186 featured a badge reflecting their naval aviation status – an anchor and winged helmet. They retained both badge and unit code 'J9' for much of their subsequent wartime career as part of III./StG 1.

Ju 87B-1 'S2+NN' of 5./StG 77, Neudorf, September 1939

Another II.*Gruppe* machine as witness the red trim, this B-1 carries standard early wartime markings and the 5.*Staffel* badge of the Polish campaign period. This latter emblem consisted of a hare, wearing a Polish army cap, about to be hit by a bomb.

Ju 87B-1 'Yellow A/NO+HP' of FFS(C) 12, Prague-Ruzyne, 1941

In contrast, and representative of ex-operational aircraft relegated to training duties after the outbreak of war, this 'Berta', once of III./StG 2 (note the Hlinka Cross *Gruppe* badge), and now serving with *Fliegerführerschule* (C)12 (Advanced Training School 12) at Prague, has reverted to a four-letter code (possibly its original *Stammkenn-zeichen* – the basic identity code allocated to each aircraft upon manufacture), augmented by a yellow 'A' for in-school identification.

Oberleutenant Bruno Dilley, *Staffelkapitän* of 3./StG 1 is seen wearing the multi-zippered summer flying suit and early-style kapok life-jacket as used in 1939-40. Note also the officer's field cap (*Fliegermütze*) and cloth patch on his right sleeve denoting rank. Dilley survived the war having flown some 650 combat missions.

Leutnant Hermann Haas was the *Ketten-führer* of the original trio of Ju 87s sent to Spain, and he is shown here in *Condor Legion* dress and standard Luftwaffe flying boots of the period. The two stars of a '*Teniente*' are worn on his cap and left breast (all Luftwaffe personnel were promoted one rank during their period of service in Spain), whilst the Nationalist flying badge is displayed on the right breast – the whole being set off with sunglasses and holstered Walther 7.65 mm P.P. pistol.

After commanding I./StG 2 'Immelmann' in Poland, Major Oskar Dinort served as *Geschwaderkommodore* of StG 2 from October 1939 through to October 1941. Well-known throughout the Luftwaffe, 'Uncle Oskar' also survived the war, latterly as the CO of a training division. Here he wears an outfit similar to Dilley's, albeit with flying helmet, throat microphone and later style inflatable life-jacket. Note also the cloth rank patch.

The first NCO of the entire Luftwaffe to be awarded the Knight's Cross (on 8/5/40), Unteroffizier Gerhard Grenzel of I./StG 1 wears a standard issue flying blouse (*Flieger-bluse*) with leather helmet and other ranks' belt, plus obligatory Walther 7.65 mm P.P. pistol. Note Unteroffizier collar patches and shoulder straps. Grenzel failed to return from an attack on a Malta convoy on 10/1/41.

Oberst Günther Schwartzkopff, *Geschwader-kommodore* of StG 77, was killed in action over France on 14/5/40. He too is wearing summer flying overalls, but combines these with officer's service cap and belt. Note the Oberst's rank patch prominently displayed on his right sleeve.

Schwartzkopff's successor at the head of StG 77 was Major Clemens Graf von Schönborn-Wiesentheid (ex-*Kommandeur* of III./StG 2). Shown in full officer's service dress, he is wearing the Knight's Cross awarded on 21 July 1940. After leading StG 77 in the Balkans and Russia, von Schönborn-Wiesentheid was appointed chief of the Luftwaffe mission in Bulgaria, where he was killed in the crash of a Fieseler *Storch* on 30 August 1944.

BLITZKRIEG: THE LOW COUNTRIES AND FRANCE

The months of uneasy calm which settled over the western front following the subjugation of Poland - the so-called 'Phoney War' - saw little significant action as both sides busied themselves in preparation, the Anglo-French by manning their defences whilst the Germans gathered their forces for the attack. For the Luftwaffe the winter of 1939-40 was a period of rapid expansion, the numbers of both *Jagd-* and *Kampfgruppen* increasing by more than 50 per cent between September 1939 and May 1940 (from 18 to 29 and from 30 to 46 respectively).

It was all the more surprising then, given their success in Poland, that not a single new *Stukagruppe* was created during this period. There was, however, a significant organisational change. Rather than dividing the Stukas evenly among the commands, as had been the case in Poland, two-thirds of their number were now concentrated in a single specialised corps.

The planned assault in the west was divided into two distinct stages. Operation *Yellow* was to open with an all-out attack on Belgium and Holland, its aim being to draw the British and northern French armies out of their prepared positions along Belgium's western borders, and bring them forward to the aid of the two endangered neutral countries. Once the Allies were out in the open and on the move north-eastwards, the major German thrust would be delivered to their rear, with armoured divisions sweeping around behind them and driving hard for the Channel coast. This would effectively isolate the northernmost Anglo-French forces in the Low Countries, which could then be defeated separately. Once this was accomplished the bulk of the *Wehrmacht* could launch the second phase of the campaign – Operation *Red* – the advance across the Somme, through the French heartland down to the Spanish and Swiss frontiers.

Signallers of an air landing unit wave greetings to one of the Stukas which provided them with such effective close support during their initial airborne assault on the Low Countries

Generalfeldmarschall Hermann Göring, Luftwaffe C-in-C, visits I./StG 77 at their Radom base on 13 September. Among the high-ranking officers in attendance may be seen Generalmajor Wolfram *Freiherr* von Richthofen (OC of *Fliegerführer* z.b.V.), General Erhard Milch (Luftwaffe Inspector General) and Generalmajor Hans Jeschonnek (Chief of the Luftwaffe General Staff)

By the end of the campaign III./StG 2 'Immelmann' had been transferred south from Stolp, in Pommerania, to Vienne, in Slovakia. Here, at the foot of the High Tatra mountains, their purpose was to prevent the escape southwards of the last remnants of the Polish army. 8.*Staffel* unloads stores and provisions brought in by Ju 52 transports

The engine of this 8.*Staffel* machine gets a test run after having had some minor combat damage repaired

The Stukas move up into Belgium. A Ju 87B-1 of StG 2 'Immelmann' rests awhile at St Trond, flanked by the skeletal remains of a pair of Belgian Air Force Fiat C.R.42 biplane fighters

The spearheading VIII.*Fliegerkorps* would be heavily involved in all stages of this ambitious timetable. The months of March and April 1940 were therefore filled with a series of manoeuvres and dress rehearsals preparing the Stuka crews for the starring roles they were about to play. The key to the entire operation was the huge Belgian fort of Eben Emael. Built into the near-vertical sides of the Albert Canal (itself, in effect, an enormous 38-metre deep anti-tank ditch), the guns of the fort dominated the local countryside, including the Dutch border town of Maastricht and three vital bridges. These provided the axes for the 'feint' attack on Belgium. If Eben Emael could not be neutralised at once – essentially if its heavy guns remained intact to destroy the bridges – the whole edifice of the plan of campaign would crumble.

Even against such antiquated fortresses as Modlin and Oscarsborg the effect of Stuka bombardment had not been immediate. And Eben Emael was a far tougher proposition altogether. Completed only five years earlier, its three underground levels were topped by massive concrete casemates, heavily armoured dome-shaped steel cupolas and batteries of anti-aircraft guns. With an authorised strength of 1200 officers and men, Eben Emael was considered impregnable. Yet, as it transpired, the fortress was captured by just 78 airborne troops landing by glider on its grassy surface area at dawn on 10 May 1940 in a now historic *coup de main.* Armed with revolutionary hollow-shaped charges, they set about disabling the armoured gun emplacements. The door for Operation *Yellow* was open.

Also aloft at first light that day, the Stukas had no less an important role to perform. While waves of Ju 87s of StG 2 pounded the peripheral defences of the fort and the nearby village of Eben Emael to prevent reinforcements from reaching its west-facing entrance tunnel, four of their number pin-pointed a building in the village of Lanaeken, some 14 kilometres along the Albert Canal to the north. This was the headquarters of the Belgian officer responsible for ordering the demolition of the three canal bridges should they appear to be in danger of falling into German hands. The weeks of practice which the four pilots had put in for this one attack paid off. The HQ was blasted into rubble before the *Commandant* could transmit the necessary orders.

Despite the subsequent confusion one bridge was blown up in the face of the advancing Germans. Troops poured across the other two. In the days ahead these structures would become the target for near-suicidal Allied bombing attacks and provide the setting for the RAF's first two VCs of World War 2.

While the now Major Dinort's StG 2 was thus engaged against the Albert Canal and its defences, StG 77, led by Oberst Günter Schwartzkopff, had taken off from Cologne-Butzweilerhof to attack other frontier fortifications along the River Meuse to the south around Liège. That evening the two *Geschwader* combined forces to mount a major dive-bombing raid on the port of Antwerp.

The opening day of the invasion had cost over a dozen Stukas, most of

One of the forts along the Meuse, possibly Flémalle itself, bears the scars of a concentrated Stuka attack while the surrounding orchards and countryside remain unscathed

A mix of dining-room chairs and deckchairs for this group of officers of 10.(St)/LG 1 relaxing over a game of chess. 'Cäsar-Ulrich' ('L1+CU') waits patiently in the background, but the pile of beer glasses on the table presumably indicates no more flying today!

them from Dinort's *Gruppen* (including seven from the subordinate I./StG 76 alone) and all to anti-aircraft fire. Twenty-four hours later it was the turn of Allied fighters to inflict casualties among the ranks of the Ju 87s. And again it was StG 2 which bore the brunt.

The first air battle of the campaign in the west erupted just east of Brussels when some 60 Ju 87s of StG 2 were attacked by six RAF Hurricane Is of No 87 Sqn. It was in the ensuing melée between Tirlemont and St Trond that the Stuka's basic flaws – its deficiencies in speed, armour and defensive armament – were first brought home to the men flying it. Despite forming a defensive circle (a manoeuvre in itself a tacit admission of inferiority), they forfeited six of their number, plus another damaged. It was only the Allies' own growing confusion and disorganisation in the weeks of withdrawals and retreat to come that would save them from even heavier losses.

For the push across Belgium had already begun. Among the first units to move into occupied territory were elements of StG 77. IV.(St)/LG 1 were ordered forward to Bierset, west of Liège, on only the second day of the fighting – it was a calculated risk which very nearly came to grief. The ground echelon had just begun to clear the field of debris from the opening day's bombing raids when they came under fire from the guns of Fort Flémalle, one of Liège's outer ring of fortifications.

Fortunately, the *Gruppenkommandeur* himself landed at Bierset during a lull in the bombardment. After being appraised of the situation, he took off to lead IV.(St)/LG 1 in an attack on the offending fort, just visible on the horizon. The action that followed moments later afforded the ground personnel a grandstand view of the destructive power wielded by an

A mechanic checks the glycol level of a Ju 87B-1. Groundcrews were able to witness at first hand the destructive power and pinpoint accuracy of their charges as Stukas battered Belgian defences in full view of their own forward landing grounds

All is ready. The groundcrews can relax, the aircraft tarpaulined and camouflaged, as a group of officers (right) await further orders

unopposed *Stukagruppe* in full cry. The fort gave them no more trouble, although it would not be until 17 May, and in the wake of a further attack by StG 2, that Flémalle finally surrendered, being one of the last of the Liège forts to do so. By that time the Germans had entered Brussels, but not without further losses to StG 2 on the way, as Oberleutnant Lothar Lau, Kapitän of 8.*Staffel*, recounts:

'We are briefed to attack road and rail targets between Tirlemont and Louvain. Unusually favourable weather; three-tenths cloud in an otherwise perfectly blue May sky. I lead my two *Kettenhunde* (wingmen) towards Tirlemont. Let's see what's happening at the railway station. Nothing doing. We've been here once today already. Troops of all kinds are streaming into town from the east. Climb over the southern suburbs for a quick look at the airfield, but the nest is empty. So back to a large cross-roads on the eastern edge of town, dive gently without using the brakes and plant our bomb smack in the middle of the crossing. "The whole corner house has collapsed into the street!" reports my wireless-operator excitedly.

'Out over the rooftops followed by machine-gun fire. Suddenly a loud bang. Then two more in quick succession. I recognise that noise from Poland. We've been hit. It suddenly smells strongly of petrol. And there, in the wing, the jagged exit holes are clearly visible.

'The rest of the *Staffel* are still west of town, my two *Kettenhunde* several streets away. Another hit knocks out the radio. I give the signal to re-form but everybody is too busy to notice. I circle, but my fuel is running out fast. So we set off alone, hedge-hopping eastwards at ground level.

'St Trond comes into sight, we pass it to the south. After a while the unmistakable silhouette of the cathedral at Tongres. Once past that and we're home and dry. The leading *Panzers* are already pushing south-westwards out of Tongres. Set course for Maastricht - maybe we can even make it as far as Aachen!

'Suddenly the voice of the wireless-operator in my earphones: "Enemy fighters, two Hurricanes!" My question, are they attacking us, is drowned out by the racket from the rear cockpit as he opens fire. Now at least I know! I try to use every dip in the ground and scrap of cover I can find. My wireless-operator calls out the direction of the attack each time the enemy closes in for the kill.

'I heave the machine to left and right, always turning into the side the attack is coming from, but all the while slowly gaining a little more ground eastwards. We take more hits. The two *Engländer* have me well and truly boxed in: if I turn towards one, the other lets fly at me with all he's got.

'Bullets fly past either side of me. More strikes in the fuselage. My wireless-operator is hit. In the mirror I can see him slumped over his gun. Again the machine shudders under a hail of fire – the elevators don't respond any more. Blood is flowing down the side of my face. The engine has been hit too – it's coughing badly and oil covers the windscreen.

'I shout to the wireless-operator: "Hang on. We're going down!" An automatic grab at the brakes and flaps. I use the rudder to try to steer the machine between the fruit trees directly ahead of us. We make it. I clamber out and pull the unconscious wireless-operator clear. The first ground troops are soon on the scene and an ambulance is quickly organised to take him to hospital in Maastricht. But my trusty old "Anton-Siegfried"

Already bombed-up, Ju 87B-2 'T6+HL of 3./StG 2 'Immelmann' undergoes last-minute preparations for its next sortie

is a sorry sight in the middle of the orchard, fuselage broken in two, half of one wing missing and the nose pointing up at the still, clear, blue sky.'

With the crew now aboard and the thin screen of camouflage branches removed (but with the makeshift chocks still in place) 'Heinrich-Ludwig's' engine is cranked up. Note that the *Staffel* badge is carried on both sides of the fuselage below the windscreen, but that the aircraft's individual letter 'H' is repeated on the front of the starboard wheelspat only – incidentally, the yellow-tipped spinner on this machine appears to have taken a nasty knock!

As soon as the northern Anglo-French forces were fully committed to their advance into central Belgium, the main blow fell. German armoured columns burst out of the 'impenetrable' Ardennes to the south and raced for the one obstacle in their path – the River Meuse at Sedan. Once that had been crossed the way to the Channel coast would be wide open.

The whole of VIII.*Fliegerkorps* was temporarily seconded to *Luftflotte* 3 for the attack on French positions guarding the Meuse crossings. On 13 May they struck. In just five hours that day StG 77 alone flew more than 200 individual sorties. Towards evening the weather closed in and flying was restricted, but by that stage the Stukas had done their job. The combined onslaught from the air and from the ground – the ear-splitting wail of engines and sirens from the diving Stukas overhead punctuating the constant rumble of Panzer and artillery fire from across the river – had completely demoralised the French defenders. Within 48 hours the Meuse had been successfully breached.

14 May over the Sedan bridgeheads has gone down in Luftwaffe history as the 'Day of the Fighters', the *Jagdwaffe*'s Bf 109s annihilating the Allied bombers attempting to deny the crossings to the advancing Germans. The *Stukagruppen*, too, also suffered casualties along the Meuse on that date (11 aircraft fell to flak or Allied fighters), with no single loss being more keenly felt than that of Oberst Günter Schwartzkopff, *Kommodore* of StG 77, whose Ju 87 received a direct hit from French anti-aircraft fire over Le Chesne near Sedan. Schwartzkopff's untiring efforts before the war in promoting the dive-bomber's cause had earned him the title of 'The father of the Stukas'. His dedicated service since, which had seen him at the head of StG 77 during every major action in Poland and the west to date, being recognised by posthumous promotion to Generalmajor and the award of the Knight's Cross.

On 18 May another, more familiar, name associated with the Stuka also received the Knight's Cross. Ironically, Generalmajor Wolfram *Freiherr* von Richthofen, World War 1 fighter pilot and cousin of the legendary 'Red Baron', had voiced strong opposition to the dive-bomber back in 1936 while serving as head of development of the *Technisches Amt* (Technical office) under the flamboyant Ernst Udet. Nor was he overly enamoured of the Ju 87's performance in Spain three years later when C-in-C of the *Legion Condor*. Yet, it was this self-same machine which, under von Richthofen's overall command, had paved the way for victory in Poland, and was even now carving a swathe through northern France.

For with the broad waters of the Meuse behind them, the five Panzer divisions of 12.*Armee*, supported by von Richthofen's VIII.*Fliegerkorps*, had their sights firmly set on the Channel coast. The armoured dash across France during that third week of May 1940 – the very epitome of *Blitzkrieg* – was perhaps the Stuka's 'finest hour'. Responding to the Panzers' every call, they cleared pockets of potential resistance ahead of the route of advance, broke up the Allied tank attacks along its flanks, harried rear-area reinforcements – many of whom were filled with dread by the mere mention of the word 'Stuka' – and spread panic along the refugee-filled roads.

In order to keep abreast of the advancing ground forces, the *Stukagruppen* were constantly moving forward, taking up residence on anything suitable, from an abandoned enemy airfield to a level patch of cow pasture. 'Bertas' often found themselves operating at the very limit of their range, and the timely arrival of the first Ju 87Rs at this juncture provided a source of much needed, longer-legged, reinforcement.

At the height of the advance, while brushing aside the remnants of French Gen Bruneau's 1st Armoured Division outside St Quentin, the *Blitzkrieg* steamrollered over the very area where Harry Brown's little S.E.5a had first dive-bombed in anger some 22 years earlier. On 18 May StG 2 twice attacked troop trains in Soissons station, whilst 24 hours later their bombs not only blocked the exits from Amiens but also broke up a counter-attack by French tanks outside Laon.

On 20 May spearheads of the 2.*Panzerdivision* reached the Channel. The British and Belgian armies, plus a large number of French troops, were now isolated within a large pocket with their backs against the sea around Dunkirk. While some *Stukagruppen* concentrated on reducing the perimeter of this pocket, preventing any attempts at breaking out southwards to rejoin the main body of French forces, others began to invest the Channel ports.

On the Belgian (eastern) flank of the pocket other *Gruppen* were attacking the Armentières-Estaires-Bailleul triangle where enemy troops were so thick on the ground that veterans of the Polish campaign likened the scene below to that along the Bzura eight months earlier.

Meanwhile, the Channel ports were being rolled up one by one as the Panzers advanced northwards along the coast from the mouth of the Somme. Boulogne was occupied on 25 May after heavy raids by II./StG2

Ju 87B-2s of I./StG 77 stand camouflaged among the trees bordering the field at Courcelles, near St Quentin ready for the second phase of the campaign against France

and I. (St)/TrGr 186. The next day it was the turn of Calais, when the remnants of the Rifle Brigade, holed up in the town's Citadel, were forced to surrender after a 'horrific Stuka bombardment' by StGs 2 and 77.

Over the next few days, for the first time since the start of the campaign in the west, the *Stukagruppen* would again suffer heavily. But one unidentified pilot, obviously an ex-*Condor Legion* man, had a lucky escape.

Despite the success of the *Blitzkrieg* in western Europe, the Stukas had paid a price. In addition to some 120 aircraft lost or written-off during the campaign, many more were damaged. This machine of StG 2, sieved by bullet holes and shrapnel and minus its landing gear fairings and all other unnecessary weight, is setting off back to Germany for repair. The journey will have to be made in short hops, for every fuel tank except one has been shot to pieces

'We were somewhere over Calais in our *Jolanthe* with orders to drop our "big one" on the Citadel. But that's no easy job when you've got three English fighters sitting on your tail. They had appeared out of nowhere from a cloud and had already turned my starboard wing into a sieve. *"Ei, Donnerwetter"*, I thought, "three fighters, that makes 25 machine guns – and all shooting at me". Old *Jolanthe* had caught quite a packet. And to make matters worse my gunner had been wounded...'

He nevertheless managed to escape further damage and get away, only for his engine to give up. He began to glide inland:

'...after a few kilometres – we were quite low by then – I saw the recognitition panels of a German infantry unit laid out in a large field. The machine landed heavily and immediately somersaulted over onto its back. That told yours truly something that hadn't been apparent before – the tyres had been shot to pieces too!

'My gunner and I were trapped underneath the machine in a somewhat uncomfortable position and unable to move. But we soon heard sounds of spades and shovels and ten minutes later we were on our way, still a bit groggy, to the field hospital. The MO patched us up with all the usual sympathy of a frontline medic – "Some people are just too spupid to get themselves killed" – and next day we were in a transport Ju heading for hospital back in Germany.'

There now remained just the one prize to complete Operation *Yellow* – Dunkirk.

Although some rear echelon troops and other supernumeraries had already begun returning to England as early as 20 May, Operation *Dynamo* – the planned evacution of the BEF – was not officially put into effect until the evening of 26 May. That same day Göring had ordered his Luftwaffe to make Dunkirk its priority target. The beginning of the evacuation in earnest thus coincided with an escalation of the previous days' air attacks. At dawn on 27 May two *Kampfgeschwader* mounted a raid on the town and port, and later in the day the *Stukagruppen* added their weight to the assault, one of their victims being a large French cross-Channel steamer.

The weather favoured the Allies for the next 36 hours, low cloud and rain over the target area and beyond greatly reduced the Luftwaffe's effectiveness. But by the afternoon of 29 May conditions had improved sufficiently to allow full-scale air operations to resume:

'The bad weather meant that we hadn't been able to "lay our morning eggs" – our description for the first sortie of the day – but now fresh orders had arrived by messenger. Target Dunkirk!

'Dark columns of smoke show us the way, although it still isn't ideal Stuka weather. Huge banks of clouds reaching down almost to ground level greatly hamper downward visibility. As we each try to keep in touch with the man in front through the scudding cloud and smoke from the burning town, red tramlines of tracer from the light flack combine with explosions from heavier calibre guns to create an almost impenetrable curtain.

'The machine in front of me tips slowly onto its nose and disappears into its dive. At that moment I spot a gap in the clouds and see beneath me a harbour wall, a large loading ramp and – I can hardly believe my eyes – a nice fat freighter tied up alongside. I run my hands over the controls almost by instinct. Now it's just stick forward, and the old crate stands on its head as down we go straight at the target.

'An absolute wall of flak comes up at me. Quickly, a few random bursts from my wing guns in reply. I align the machine onto the target, take careful aim through the sight and release my bomb. While recovering, I look back to check the result – where the ramp had been there is now a rising column of fire and smoke.'

This combined attack by three *Stukagruppen* had been concentrated on the Dunkirk mole, which was packed with ships busily embarking troops. The destroyer HMS *Grenade* was sunk and others hit and badly damaged. Many smaller merchant vessels were also lost, including the Thames paddle-steamer *Crested Eagle.* As a result, no further major evacuation attempts were made from the mole, the bulk of the remaining troops being lifted straight off the beaches.

Another spell of bad weather kept the Stukas grounded for the last two days of May, but on 1 June they were back again with a vengeance. In a series of raids lasting all day, they took a heavy toll of Allied shipping. One pilot managed to plant his bomb straight down the aft funnel of HMS *Keith*, one of three RN destroyers sunk off Dunkirk that day, whilst others went after the merchantmen.

This second phase of the *Wehrmacht's* almost clinical invasion and defeat of metropolitan France was launched on 5 June. For von Richthofen's Stukas, the next fortnight degenerated into a series of dashes to, and across, one river line after the other as the French retreat gathered momentum. Initially tasked with supporting the armour of *Panzergruppe* von Kleist across the Somme between Amiens and Péronne, and with assisting 9.*Armee's* breaking through the Weygand Line around Laon, VIII.*Fliegerkorps* was then to cover the spearheads of 2.*Armee* down to the Swiss border.

The first 72 hours saw the French thrown back across the Somme, the Oise and the Aisne as the Panzers raced for the next natural great water barrier, the River Marne, east of Paris. The *Stukagruppen* were in constant attendance, on call to strike at the first signs of any organised enemy resistance, and attacking bridges to disrupt the French lines of retreat. A German war correspondent gave a graphic account of one such sortie flown on 7 June:

'Yesterday, we were over one of the main assembly points for enemy troops – a town some ten minutes' flying time east of Paris, which was just visible through the layer of smoke and haze which covers every large city.

'Our *Kette* kept tight formation as we approached the target. Others flew to the left and right of us. '"Fasten your harness, we're diving!" the pilot called out. It was almost as if – for a split second – the machine hung motionless in the sky. Then the tail rose almost vertically as the nose tipped earthwards. The flow of air built up, whistling over the wing surfaces and beating against the cabin windows. The ground – a moment ago a relief model unfolding below us with contours, hills and a horizon – was suddenly a flat map filling our entire field of vision . . . a map whose details were growing sharper and larger by the second!

'The pilot hung motionless in his seat, his right eye pressed against the sight as he concentrated on the target. The howl of the engine rose and drowned the noise of the wind. There's the bridge! His finger pressed the button on the control column marked with the word "Bombs". A slight jolt. On either side of us, swaying gently only some 30 metres away, the two *Kettenhunde* released their bombs in perfect unison.

The detritus of Dunkirk. Wrecked Austin vehicles of the BEF, immobilised and abandoned on the cratered and littered beach. The three-funnelled vessel in the background with its bow blown off is the 1278-ton French destroyer *l'Adroit*, sunk and stranded by air attack on 21 May

'At almost the same moment I was pressed down hard in my seat as the pilot began to pull out. I swallowed to relieve the pressure in my ears. The wings flexed slightly. Then we were flying horizontally, but jinking to the left and right, rising and falling, to throw the enemy flak gunners off their aim as we reformed for the homeward flight. Three hours later aerial photographs showed the bridge to be completely destroyed.'

On 12 June the Germans crossed the Marne near Château-Thierry. The next day Paris was declared an open city. Despite the growing confusion of the French retreat, the *Stukagruppen* continued to encounter small pockets of individual resistance, both on the ground and in the air, as they swept southwards past France's undefended capital off to their right. I./StG 2 had already destroyed some 20 to 30 tanks gathering to launch a counter-attack on the Germans' unprotected flank to the north of the city. On 13 June a *Staffel* of StG 77, based south-east of Soissons, was ordered to attack the railway line between Troyes and Auxerre. They had just flown over the leading Panzers near Montmirail when:

'. . . something caught the *Staffelkapitän's* attention; small dots in the distance far ahead. He watched the gaggle of tiny specks swooping and diving among the clouds. Must be our fighter escort, he thought. "They're in a good mood today!" he said to his wireless-operator... The light suddenly dawns: they're French! "Haven't seen so many Frenchmen since Sedan", the *Staffelkapitän* thinks to himself as the wireless-operator opens fire. The smell of cordite fills the cabin. The *Kapitän* waits until he sees the lines of tracer shooting past. Now! "Turn into them!" As one, his pilots – veterans all – bank towards the enemy fighters and open fire with their wing guns. It was a manoeuvre they had thoroughly practised all winter long back in Cologne – practised until they were heartily sick of it. But now it was paying dividends.'

Taken by surprise, the French fighters were forced to break to avoid the oncoming Stukas. As they flashed past each other the Stukas' rear gunners let fly, claiming at least two of the enemy which were seen going down trailing smoke. But it was the arrival of the Bf 109 escort which saved the Ju 87s from further attack (and almost certain losses), and which accounted for nine of the French Moranes.

Forty-eight hours later the whole of I./StG 77 was back over the Auxerre region bombing and strafing a stubborn nest of French troops holed up in a group of fortified buildings. On 16 June the Germans crossed the Seine. The next day, despite unseasonably bad weather, the Stukas were attacking enemy columns around Dijon and supporting bridgeheads over the River Loire near Nevers.

The end was now in sight. Marshal Pétain had appealed for an armistice on 17 June – that day too German reconnaissance aircraft reported no large enemy formations along the Loire or Saône rivers, or anywhere beyond right up to the Swiss border.

On 18 June von Richthofen ordered two-thirds of VIII.*Fliegerkorps* to stand down, although signs of renewed French activity north of Dijon later in the day resulted in a last flurry of Stuka attacks, and the reported surrender of three French divisions soon afterwards.

Ironically, 18 June also witnessed the final Ju 87 losses of the entire campaign when two aircraft of III./StG 51 collided over Nivelles – the last of some 120 Stukas lost to all causes since 10 May.

By 19 June VIII.*Fliegerkorps* was being held at readiness on bases around the Nevers-Auxerre areas of central France. However, the mission scheduled for the following day was cancelled, the advance halted, and the ground forces withdrawn to the newly agreed demarcation line between occupied and unoccupied (Vichy) France. Forty-eight hours later the Armistice was signed at Compiègne.

And so the Stukas never made it to the Swiss border. Instead they were ordered to execute another 180° turn, for while much of the Luftwaffe retired to the Homeland for a well deserved and much needed rest and refit, von Richthofen's VIII.*Fliegerkorps* were to put their proven precision attack capabilities to another, more immediate, use. In the last weeks of June they headed back up to France's battle-scarred northern coast, their new task, to close the English Channel to British shipping.

A direct hit scored by I.StG 77 on one of the 'little ships' taking part in the Dunkirk evacuation on 1 June 1940. Note the near misses of the *Kettenhunde* aft of the stricken vessel

THE MYTH IS EXPLODED

On 4 July, III./StG 51 staged a maximum-effort raid on Portland harbour that resulted in probably the highest military loss of life ever inflicted by a single air attack on the British Isles. Led by their new *Kommandeur*, Hauptmann Anton Keil, some 33 Stukas dived out of the morning mist, which hung over the naval base. They concentrated their attacks on the largest vessel in the harbour, the 5582-ton auxiliary anti-aircraft ship HMS *Foylebank*, and within eight minutes 22 bombs had struck the ship, killing 176 of her crew. Among them was Leading Seaman Jack Mantle who, despite being mortally wounded, continued to fire his two-pounder 'pom-pom' gun as the ship settled beneath him – an action which was recognised by the award of a posthumous VC.

StG 77 flew its first mission of the campaign on the eve of the 'official' battle when 27 aircraft of I. *Gruppe* took off from Théville late in the afternoon of 9 July to attack a convoy off Portland. They succeeded in damaging a small Ministry of Shipping vessel, but this time the Ju 87s were intercepted by three fighters – Spitfire Is of No 609 Sqn's Green Section, up from their nearby satellite airfield at Warmwell, the bulk of the unit being situated back at Middle Wallop. Engaged by the Stukas' escort of Bf 110Cs, the Spitfires claimed a solitary dive-bomber shot down.

The single kill fell to future ace Flg Off David M Crook:

'I was in an ideal position to attack and opened fire and put the remainder of my ammunition – about 2000 rounds – into him at very close range. Even in the heat of the moment I well remember my amazement at the shattering effect of my fire. Pieces flew off his fuselage and cockpit covering, a stream of smoke appeared from the engine, and a moment

. . . all is well and the bomb-laden aircraft commence their widely spaced take-off runs. Many *Stukagruppen* paraded the unit standard and provided a ceremonial honour-guard such as seen here at the beginning of each operational mission

later a great sheet of flame licked down out from the engine cowling and he dived down vertically. The flames enveloped the whole machine and he went straight down, apparently quite slowly, for about 5000 ft, till he was just a shapeless burning mass of wreckage.

'Absolutely fascinated by the sight, I followed him down, and saw him hit the sea with a great burst of white foam. He disappeared immediately, and apart from a green patch in the water there was no sign that anything had happened. The crew made no attempt to get out, and they were obviously killed in my first burst of fire.'

David Crook's premier combat victory had inflicted a grievous blow to I./StG 77, for the aircraft shot down into the Channel was being piloted by their *Kommandeur*, Hauptmann Friedrich-Karl *Freiherr* von Dalwigk zu Lichtenfels. Another of the Stuka arm's 'Old Guard', he had joined the then StG 162 'Immelmann' back in 1936. Assuming command of I./StG 77 shortly before the outbreak of war, he had personally flown at the head of the *Gruppe* on almost every one of its missions since. His 'leadership by example' throughout the Polish and French campaigns was to result in the posthumous award of the Knight's Cross and his promotion to Major.

Forty-eight hours later the Stukas were back over Portland. A ten-aircraft strong sortie despatched from the Cherbourg peninsula early on the morning of 11 July had attacked a convoy in Lyme Bay, sunk one of the escort (HMS Warrior II, a 36-year-old armed yacht) and returned without loss thanks to the efforts of their Bf 109E escorts, who downed two Spitfire Is (of No 609 Sqn again) and a solitary Hurricane I (of No 501 Sqn) during the course of the mission. No doubt encouraged by this, the *Gruppe* staged a second mission a few hours later, which comprised a mixed formation of some 20 *'Bertas'* and *'Richards'* of III./StG 2, escorted by twice that number of Bf 110Cs from III./ZG 76. The Stukas had just completed their dives against a convoy off Portland, and were at their most vulnerable, when they were intercepted at low-level by six Hurricane Is of No 601 Sqn, which had been scrambled from Tangmere, some 50 miles further east.

Again, the RAF fighters arrived too late to stop the Stukas from completing their attack, and just one machine would fail to return, having been sent crashing into the water alongside Portland mole after being attacked by one-time Olympic skiier, Flg Off G N S Cleaver, who also claimed a He 111 near Portsmouth on this date. No less than four of the Bf 110 escorts were lost as they fought a bitter rearguard action in the Stukas' wake against a number of Hurricanes sent to reinforce No 601 Sqn.

While VIII.*Fliegerkorps* was thus directing its attention against the Dorset coast and the western end of the Channel, the two *Stukagruppen* now subordinated to *Luftflotte* 2 and based to the east in the Pas de Calais were awaiting the opportunity to attack across the Channel's narrowest point – the Straits of Dover.

Their chance came on 13 July when reports were received of a convoy attempting to run the gauntlet of the Straits. While a bitter dogfight raged between the three *Staffeln* of Bf 109Es from JG 51 and 11 Hurricane Is of No 56 Sqn, the Stukas managed to deliver their ordnance and then escape without loss, although two machines received slight damage – in an early example of the overclaiming that was to plague Fighter Command during

Hauptmann Anton Keil, *Gruppenkommandeur* of II./StG 1 (the ex-III./StG 51), is seen here wearing the Knight's Cross which was awarded to him on 19 August 1940. Keil remained at the head of II./StG 1 until he was killed on the Eastern Front a year later when his aircraft overturned during an emergency landing on swampy ground

Unlike Keil, Helmut Mahlke, who commanded III./StG 1 throughout the Battle of Britain and beyond, survived two crash landings in Russia. He is pictured here later in the war as an Oberstleutnant on the staff of *Luftflotte* 6

As the port wingman closes up on his leader, the badge of III.*Gruppe* (the Hlinka Cross of Slovakia, bestowed by the local population during the unit's brief sojourn at Vienne the previous autumn) is clearly apparent

the Battle of Britain, the Hurricane squadron (who lost two pilots to the Bf 109 escort) claimed to have shot down seven Ju 87s during the course of this sortie.

Twenty-four hours later an attack on a convoy off Eastbourne by all three *Staffeln* of IV.(St)/LG 1 fared less well, with one Stuka and one of the escorting Bf 109s being lost to RAF fighters.

Nearly a week was to pass before II./StG 1 reappeared off the Kent coast. In the early evening of 20 July they attacked an eastbound convoy, code-named 'Bosom', as it approached the Straits of Dover. Once again a strong fighter escort (over 50 Bf 109s and Bf 110s) proved its worth, for despite being bounced out of the sun by Hurricane Is of Nos 32 and 615 Sqns, plus Spitfire Is of Nos 65 and 610 Sqn, all Hauptmann Keil's pilots again made it safely back to France (albeit this time with four aircraft damaged and one gunner wounded – the Hurricane pilots claimed to have downed two Stukas), having sunk the coaster *Pulborough* and left the destroyer HMS *Brazen* with her back broken. The fighter escorts faired less well, however, losing five Bf 109Es in a swirling dogfight that lasted over 30 minutes.

Five days later the Stukas suffered their first multiple losses of the Battle when missions were flown over both ends of the Channel. Between Dover and Folkestone a series of heavy attacks on a westbound convoy by units of *Luftflotte* 2, including II./StG 1 and IV.(St)/LG 1, sank five ships and damaged four others, including the destroyers *Boreas* and *Brilliant.* A pilot of II./StG 1 described the scene:

'The French coast slips away behind us. While our fighter escort banks and turns all around us we keep in tight formation, heading out over the gently rolling sea towards our target. The first faint outline of England is already visible when we locate the remains of the convoy. A few scattered ships are trying to reach the safety of that far shore. Our comrades who were here before us have done their job well. Only eight ships are still above water.

'The *Kommandeur* gives the prearranged signal to attack. Ahead of me one machine after the other wings over and disappears into its vertical dive. I am just about to follow suit when an English fighter closes in on me. I quickly stand my crate on its head and succeed in shaking him off. While my wireless-operator watches him and keeps up

III./StG 2 'Immelmann' was heavily involved in the western Channel convoy actions of mid-July. This small coaster has had a lucky escape, as witness the rings in the water marking a succession of near misses

A *'Berta'* of 7./StG 77, its bomb racks empty, reaches the safety of the Normandy coast. Note the two machines, just visible backround left, peeling off to land

a running commentary on his movements, I concentrate on the ship I have selected as my target. It looms larger in my sights by the second. A slight pressure on the release button – a jolt – and my bomb is on its way.

'Looking back, I see it explode alongside the ship's hull. But the aircraft behind me scores a direct hit. There is no time to bask in our success – despite the best efforts of our fighter escort, enemy fighters have broken through and are trying to pick us off one by one. Diving out of the sun's glare they have caught a comrade ahead of me broadside on. Although his machine is already in flames he climbs briefly to give himself and his operator a chance to bale out. Seconds later his aircraft disappears in a column of spray.

'My own operator reports two fighters approaching. One sits on my tail while the other remains off high to one side. With one wingtip almost touching the water I bank to evade the fire from the first while my observer looses off at the second. They break away for another pass, but in the meantime I quickly tuck myself in behind a gaggle of comrades ahead of me as we head for home at full throttle.'

Two II./StG 1 machines were lost in this action and a third – of IV.(St)/LG 1 – was damaged. Meanwhile, elements of VIII.*Fliegerkorps* to the west had returned yet again to Portland. After the raid III./StG 1 was chased back across the Channel by RAF fighters. They suffered two aircraft damaged and one lost, the latter shot into the sea by two No 152 Sqn Spitfire Is just before reaching the safety of Cherbourg.

Forty-eight hours later a machine of I./StG 77 failed to return from a 30 Stuka-strong attack on convoy 'Bacon' steaming east off Portland – it was shot down into Weymouth Bay by future Hurricane ace Plt Off C T Davis of No 238 Sqn. On this same day the Royal Navy lost two more destroyers to air attack (HMSs *Codrington* and *Wren*), forcing it to withdraw its Dover flotilla to safer waters.

The weather deteriorated as July drew to a close, but the *Stukagruppen* had already performed to perfection the initial task required of them in the run-up to the planned invasion of England. By 'plugging' the Channel at either end, and neutralising the Royal Navy's south coast destroyer flotillas (which had lost a dozen vessels since mid-May, plus many others withdrawn from the area for essential repairs), they had secured the cross-Channel sealanes for the invasion fleet, which was even now being assembled in northern European ports.

Next would come stages two and three of their part in the conquest of Great Britain. In August – repeating the tactics of Poland and France – they would take out RAF Fighter Command's forward airfields in a series of precision attacks in preparation for the landings. And in September, once the German army was safely ashore, they would resume their classic role of 'flying artillery' as the ground-troops pushed northwards into the heart of England. The relative ease with which they had accomplished phase one (at a cost of only some dozen aircraft lost or written off) had given no indication of the storm that was about to break over them.

On 8 August, however, the last major convoy action of the Battle afforded a grim foretaste of things to come. Convoy CW 9 (code-named 'Peewit'), comprising 20 merchantmen and nine naval escorts, had left the Medway the previous evening, but before dawn three of its number had already been sunk by E-boats in the Straits of Dover – its progress having been tracked by the recently-installed *Freya* radar site situated on the Calais coast. As it ploughed westwards along the Channel, it was subjected to two Stuka attacks.

The first, by elements of StG 1, was intercepted and broken up by six squadrons of RAF fighters, who claimed two Ju 87s destroyed and two damaged – all these claims (plus three against Bf 109Es) were submitted by No 145 Sqn, who in turn had lost two Hurricane Is to the Stukas' escort, provided on this occasion by I./JG 27. By early afternoon 'Peewit' was off the Isle of Wight, where it was attacked by some 60 Stukas of I. and III./StG 2, backed up by I./StG 3. Despite the intervention of more fighters (18 Hurricane Is from Nos 145, 238 and 257 Sqns, plus Spitfire Is in strength from No 609 Sqn), this time the Stukas got through to the ships and sunk four and damaged seven, but lost a trio of aircraft (all from I./StG 3), with a further four suffering varying degrees of damage – two of the Ju 87s again fell to No 145 Sqn, whilst the third was claimed by No 609 Sqn. One Bf 110C of V./LG 1 and three Bf 109Es of III./JG 27 had also been lost, but they had exacted a heavy toll on the attacking Hurricane units, No 257 Sqn losing three pilots killed and No 238 Sqn two.

Of the 20 ships which had sailed from the Medway the previous night, only four arrived in Swanage virtually unscathed. The day's action had cost the four participating *Stukageschwader* nine aircraft lost or written

'Like a flock of huge birds' – a *Staffel* lifts off virtually as one to carry the fight to England's shores

off, plus a further ten damaged. By contrast, an attack by *Luftflotte* 2's two *Stukagruppen* on vessels within convoy 'Booty' off Clacton some 72 hours later resulted in their losing just one machine apiece – kills split between Nos 74 (Spitfire I) and 151 (Hurricane I) Sqns.

This latter, relatively minor, skirmish of 11 August may not in itself have been very significant in the overall scheme of the Battle, but it was to mark the start of the last week of the Stuka's operational career – and reputation – as a potent force in the skies of north-west Europe.

13 August 1940 will forever be known as '*Adlertag*' ('Eagle Day') – the opening round of the Luftwaffe's main air assault on the British Isles. For the protagonists, their 'big day' did not get off to a good start for adverse weather conditions in the early morning led to last-minute postponement orders being transmitted. But not all units received them, and in the resulting confusion some bombers flew missions devoid of fighter cover, while other fighters dutifully flew to assigned target areas without the bombers they were meant to protect!

By the afternoon, however, the weather had improved sufficiently to allow the *Stukagruppen* to launch the second phase of their three-part role in the overall invasion plan – a series of pinpoint attacks intended to neutralise Fighter Command's forward fields. They struck along both flanks of the designated assault zone. In the east *Luftflotte* 2 despatched II./StG 1 against Rochester and IV.(St)/LG 1 against Detling. The former failed to locate their target, but Hauptmann von Brauchitsch's 40 Ju 87s caused severe damage at Detling, killing 67 (including the station commander Grp Capt Edward Davis), demolishing the hangars and totally destroying 22 aircraft. Retiring without loss, IV.(St)/LG 1 landed back at Tramecourt with justifiable feelings of a job well done. It was German intelligence which was at fault – Detling was not a Fighter Command airfield.

Indeed, the only aircraft permanently based there were Anson Is of No 500 'County of Kent' Sqn, which had been seconded to Coastal Command since early 1939.

To the west, units of VIII.*Fliegerkorps* suffered similar diversities of fortune. Elements of StG 77 searched in vain for Warmwell before dropping their bombs at random over the Dorset countryside and returning to their Caen airfields unmolested. Despite being bereft of fighter cover (their 30 Bf 109 escorts from II./JG 53 had been obliged to turn back through a shortage of fuel), Hauptmann Walter Enneccerus' 27 II./StG 2 Ju 87Rs crossed the coast near Lyme Regis en route for Middle Wallop but they never made it. Intercepted by 13 Spitfire Is of No 609 Sqn, they lost five of their number in a one-sided duel over the coast, and a sixth which crashed into the Channel during the return flight – the RAF claimed to have destroyed or damaged 14 Ju 87s and Bf 109s and suffered no losses.

This decimation of the Stukas had been witnessed from the Portland cliffs by Prime Minister Winston Churchill and a clutch of senior Army generals. One of the pilots to claim a Ju 87 destroyed, and a second dive-bomber damaged, was leading No 609 Sqn ace, Flg Off John Dundas:

'Thirteen Spitfires left Warmwell for a memorable Tea-time party over Lyme Bay, and an unlucky day for the species Ju 87, of which no less than 14 suffered destruction or damage in a record squadron "bag", which also included five of the escorting Me's. The formation, consisting of about 40 dive-bombers in four-vic formation, with about as many Me 110s and

109s stepped-up above them, was surprised by 609's down-sun attack.'

The four-minute massacre off the Dorset coast was widely reported in the contemporary press, with the following headline from the 14 August 1940 edition of *The Times* being typical of those which appeared in a number of national dailies on this date;

'All the nine Junkers were brought down . . . by a single Spitfire squadron, as well as four Me 109s. This same squadron had brought down seven enemy aircraft the previous day.'

On that same 14 August *Luftflotte* 2's two *Stukagruppen* (some 80 aircraft in all, escorted by all three *Gruppen* of JG 26) again approached the Kent coast. Four RAF fighter squadrons (Hurricane Is of Nos 32 and 615 Sqns and Spitfire Is of Nos 65 and 610 Sqns – a total of 42 aircraft), alerted by radar, were waiting for them. At such short range the Messerschmitt pilots of JG 26 were able to stay and mix it, resulting in a massive dogfight involving over 200 machines developing over the coast between Dover and Folkestone. Unable to penetrate inland, the Stukas had no option but to withdraw, escaping the melée with one aircraft shot down (a 10./LG 1 machine, destroyed by a No 615 Sqn Hurricane I) and another damaged. Two *Ketten* did, however, vent their frustration on their way back to Tramecourt by bombing and sinking the unarmed Goodwin lightship. Their Bf 109 escorts were credited with destroying four British fighters for the loss a single aircraft.

The next day, the two *Gruppen* did get through to their assigned targets. Attacking Hawkinge, IV.(St)/LG 1 lost two machines to Hurricane Is of No 501 Sqn, which had been scrambled some 30 minutes earlier. Although this attack had been intercepted just as the Stukas were forming up into their pre-dive echelon, 26 Ju 87s of II./StG 1 struck the forward field of Lympne totally unopposed. Both *Gruppen* had made extensive use of smaller 50-kg fragmentation bombs, intended to destroy aircraft on the ground without rendering the fields unserviceable for future use. This time faulty intelligence could not be blamed for the fact that there were no aircraft on the ground at either airfield at the time of the attacks.

Later that same afternoon VIII.*Fliegerkorps* returned to its old stamping grounds when some 40 Ju 87Rs of I./StG 1 and II./StG 2, with a heavy escort of 60 Bf 109Es from JGs 27 and 53 and 20 Bf 110Cs from V./LG 2, set out for Portland. Engaged by Hurricane Is from No 87 and 213 Sqns and Spitfire Is from No 234 Sqn, it was again II./StG 2 which bore the brunt of the losses, three of their aircraft failing to return against I./StG 1's single casualty – three of these kills were credited to No 87 Sqn and one to No 213.

So far in this, their final week of the Battle, the Stukas had failed in their objective of forcing the RAF's fighters to abandon their forward fields. But then neither had their own losses (with the exception of Hauptmann Enneccerus' unfortunate II./StG 2) been particularly heavy. The next 72

The spells of unseasonable August weather played havoc with many of the Luftwaffe's ill-prepared forward landing grounds. I./StG 77 at le Mesul-Angat, in Normandy, did not escape their share of trouble, 1.*Staffel's* 'Dora-Heinrich' ending up on its nose after digging in a wheel upon its return from an attack on southern England. In Luftwaffe parlance, this somewhat undignified position was known as a *'Flieger-denkmal'* ('Airman's monument')

hours were to prove very different.

On 16 August it was I. and III./StG 2 which led a midday raid of over 100 aircraft (including Bf 109E escorts from II./JG 2) towards the eastern tip of the Isle of Wight. Approaching the Foreland, flares from the leading machine signalled the formation to split. While two *Ketten* of Ju 87s peeled away to port to attack the CH (Chain Home) radar station at Ventnor on the island itself (which had already been damaged by Ju 88s four days earlier), and I./StG 3 headed across Spithead towards the naval air station at Lee-on-Solent, the main body held course north-eastwards for the Fighter Command sector station at Tangmere.

Although most of the field's fighters had been scrambled, they were unable to prevent the two StG 2 *Gruppen* from carrying out a 'textbook attack'. Screaming down out of the sun high overhead, Stuka after Stuka planted its bombs with unerring accuracy. Every one of Tangmere's hangars was hit in succession, together with many of the station's other buildings and stores. A number of fighters under repair were also written off, and all eight aircraft of the nocturnal Fighter Interception Unit - seven radar-equipped Blenheims and the RAF's first Beaufighter night-fighter - were reportedly either destroyed or damaged. Twenty service and civilian personnel died amid the devastation.

The defending fighters (Hurricane Is from Nos 1, 43 and 601 Sqns and Spitfire Is of No 602 Sqn) may not have been able to forestall the onslaught, but they caught the Stukas at their most vulnerable – while recovering, attempting to regroup and trying to make good their escape. Three I. *Gruppe* Ju 87s were quickly downed by No 43 Sqn, whilst twice that number (mainly from III./StG 2) were destroyed over the Channel, the last just short of the Normandy coast. As many again, and more, were damaged, four returning to France with dead or wounded aircrew aboard (included amongst this number was a solitary I./StG 3 aircraft).

It had been a salutary lesson. The lack of a 'hostile airspace' in Spain, and the dearth of organised, and sustained, fighter opposition since, had ill-prepared the Stuka's supporters within the Luftwaffe High Command for the losses which their much-vaunted 'flying artillery' was now beginning to suffer in its new, longer-range, role. Even its staunchest advocates were having to concede that the Stuka was not operable as a strategic weapon if pitted against a determined defence – on the Tangmere raid, the Spitfire pilots of No 602 Sqn had kept the Bf 109 escorts fully occupied whilst the Hurricane units tackled the Ju 87s. It would take just one more reversal to write *finis* to its career in the west. And that reversal – even bloodier than the aftermath of Tangmere – was just 48 hours away.

After the heightened activity of the previous two days, 17 August provided a welcome lull. By day, the Luftwaffe restricted itself to reconnaissance flights, and the only combat loss was a night-intruder Ju 88 of 4./NJG 1, shot down off the Humber by a No 29 Sqn Blenheim during the early hours of the morning. However, on Sunday, 18 August, the Luftwaffe was back with a vengeance in one final attempt to destroy Fighter Command. Its main objectives were airfields, with a lesser effort being directed against the radar stations. And on this, the 'Hardest Day' of the entire Battle, none was hit harder than Major von Schönborn-Wiesentheid's *Stukageschwader* 77.

All three *Gruppen* were involved, I. and II./StG 77 (28 Stukas apiece) targeting the airfields at Thorney Island and Ford respectively, whilst III.*Gruppe* (31 aircraft) was assigned the Poling CH radar station. Reinforcing them, I./StG 3 (22 Ju 87s) was to attack the airfield at Gosport. The four *Gruppen* assembled above Cherbourg at 13.45 and then set course northwards to rendezvous with a strong escort of Bf 109E fighters (70 from JG 27 and 32 from JG 53). This was largest complement of Ju 87s (109 in total) yet seen over Britain. III./StG 77 led the way, at its head *Gruppenkommandeur* Hauptmann Helmut Bode who, having begun his flying career as a long-range maritime reconnaissance pilot, barely gave the 120-kilometre cross-Channel hop to his target a second thought. Off the eastern tip of the Isle of Wight the signal was given and the *Stukagruppen* began to peel off towards their prearranged targets.

Although some 68 RAF fighters (from Nos 601, 43, 602, 152, 234, 213 and 609 Sqns, plus two Hurricane Is from the FIU) were being vectored towards the approaching aerial armada (whose overall strength totalled four times that number), three of the four *Stukagruppen* were able to carry out their attacks unimpeded by enemy fighters. Only Hauptmann Herbert Meisel's I./StG 77 was intercepted, two squadrons of Hurricanes (Nos 43 and 601) pouncing upon them just as they were manoeuvring into position and about to dive on Thorney Island.

In the space of five minutes ten Stukas, including Meisel's, were shot down, with half as many again being damaged. Of the 56 men that had set out as I./StG 77 from Caen earlier that afternoon, some 17 were killed or mortally wounded (Meisel included), five had been made PoWs and six had returned to France with wounds.

Some 25 kilometres to the east, II./StG 77's devastating attack on Ford faced no aerial opposition. This airfield suffered heavier casualties than the three other targets combined – two hangars, the M/T park, fuel and oil tanks, stores and many other buildings were demolished, 39 aircraft damaged – 13 beyond repair – and 28 personnel killed. It was not until the Stukas were crossing back over the coast near Bognor that they were hit by the 12 Spitfire Is of No 602 Sqn that had scrambled late from Westhampnett. Two of the Ju 87s were immediately sent down into the Channel, whilst two others were damaged – one force-landed on a golf course outside Littlehampton and the other crashed near Barfleur, after struggling back to France. Losses would have been much higher had it not been for the timely intervention of the escorts from JG 27, who rapidly reduced the Spitfire squadron's complement by four.

Just across the River Arun from Ford, Poling CH radar station was the target for Major Bode's III./StG 77. His unit also attacked without hindrance from enemy fighters, but then they too ran into No 602 Sqn as they exited over Bognor in the wake of II.*Gruppe*. A single Stuka was shot down (by 7-kill ace Sgt Basil Whall – but not before Unteroffizier Schwemmer, who was manning the aircraft's flexible 7.9 mm MG 15 machine gun, had succeeded in damaging the Spitfire's engine prior to crashing to his death, along with his pilot Unteroffizier Moll, into the sea off Littlehampton. Whall managed a more successful forced landing just off the beach at Bognor Regis. Of the three damaged Stukas, one crashed in France killing both its crew.

Only the westernmost I./StG 3, targeting Gosport, succeeded in performed its attack without interference from the defenders.

A flying instructor before the war, Helmut Bode first served as a maritime reconnaissance pilot before joining the Stuka arm. He commanded III./StG 77 from its formation in 1940 until August 1942, and is portrayed here with the rank of major later in the war, wearing the Knight's Cross awarded in October 1941

Bringing up the rear of StG 77's formation on 18 August was I.*Gruppe*, commanded by Hauptmann Herbert Meisel. Assigned to attack Thorney Island, this unit lost ten Stukas to defending RAF fighters – Meisel's machine was shot into the sea off Selsey Bill

Arguably the most enduring image of the entire Battle of Britain is this machine, one of Hauptmann Meisel's luckless I./StG 77 whose final moments were caught on film as it plunged to destruction in a farmer's field outside Chichester . . .

For StG 77 the final cost of the day's action was 17 aircraft shot down or written off, with a further seven damaged. It ended at a stroke the Stuka's part in the Battle of Britain, and burst the bubble of the fearsome reputation it had built up over Poland and France. And all to little avail, for once again Luftwaffe intelligence had erred – not one of the three airfields attacked had been a Fighter Command station. At Ford, for example, the 13 machines destroyed were made up of a dozen Fleet Air Arm biplanes – five Swordfish, five Sharks and two Albacores!

After the losses of 18 August VIII.*Fliegerkorps* was transferred eastwards to the control of *Luftflotte* 2. Concentrated in the Pas de Calais, they sat out the remainder of the Battle as a sort of aeronautical 'fleet-in-being', posing a threat by their very presence, and serving to indicate to the British that the invasion was imminent. But the reality was very different. In the Battle of France the Stukas did not reach the Swiss border because they had not been required to. In the Battle of Britain they did not venture into middle England because they had not been able to. And when Operation *'Seelöwe'* ('Sea Lion') – the planned cross-Channel invasion – was quietly shelved on Hitler's orders, the bulk of the *Stukagruppen* were retired equally discreetly back to the Homeland.

A number of *Staffeln* did remain in northern France, however, and in the first half of November 1940 they staged a few sporadic anti-convoy missions around the Kent coast. The first of these, on 1 November, was mounted by 20 Ju 87Bs from the St Pol-based StG 1 against shipping in the Straits of Dover and the Thames Estuary. While their JG 26 escort managed to keep RAF fighters (Spitfires from Nos 74 and 92 Sqns) at bay, the Stukas sank two minor RN vessels, but forfeited one of their own (a 5.*Staffel* machine crewed by Gefreiters W Karrach and M Aulehner, the former being killed in the crash and the latter rescued by RN motor torpedo boat).

Six days later I./StG 3 suffered one aircraft damaged during a raid on shipping in the Thames Estuary, the Stuka's pilot, Leutenant Eberhard Morgenroth, being injured when his Stuka was attacked by No 249 Sqn Hurricane ace Plt Off T F Neil, who was credited with shooting the Ju 87B down. Gunners on the convoy escort HMS *Egret* also claimed to have shot a Stuka down during the course of the attack which saw the 1700-ton merchantman SS *Astrologer* sunk, and another vessel damaged.

A smaller number of Ju 87s from the *Gruppe* also attacked shipping off Portsmouth at around the same time as the Thames Estuary convoy was bombed, although on this occasion no vessels were hit. No 145 Sqn attempted to engage the Stukas, but were effectively driven off by Bf 109Es of I./JG 2, who downed no less than five Hurricanes from the unit in just a matter of minutes – one British pilot managed to evade the escorts and fire a few fleeting bursts at a lone Ju 87, which he claimed to have probably destroyed, but none of the Stukas involved were damaged.

On 8 November I./StG 3 and IV.(St)/LG 1 despatched some forty aircraft each (escorted by I./JG 51) against shipping along the north Kent and Essex coasts. The solitary unit defending the convoy was the Hurricane-equipped No 17 Sqn, scrambled from Martlesham Heath. The veteran pilots weighed into the Ju 87s, avoiding interception by the escorts thanks to the timely arrival of more Hurricanes from Nos 249 and 46 Sqns. Upon returning to their Suffolk base, the No 17 Sqn crews claimed to have destroyed 15 of the raiders, with five aces and the station commander, Wg Cdr A D Farquhar (also an ace), sharing the bulk of the 'kills'. In fact, only three Stukas were lost, two from 3./StG 3 and one from 12./LG 1 – all six crewmen were killed. A fourth Stuka, from 1./StG 3, force-landed at Dunkirk having run out of fuel. No ships were lost, although several were damaged including the destroyer HMS *Winchester*.

After two final raids (on 11 and 14 November over the Thames and the Straits of Dover respectively) had each cost 9./StG 1 a brace of aircraft downed and seven crewmen killed or missing, the Stukas abandoned their daylight attacks on south-east England's inshore shipping lanes.

But in December StG 1 moved up to Ostende, in Belgium, and early in the New Year the Ju 87 embarked upon the last act in its campaign against Great Britain. What was to come was a far cry from the ambitious third, and final, phase of its part in the Battle. For when, in January 1941, the Stuka reappeared over England, it was not in massed ranks of 'flying artillery' spearheading the planned invasion, but singly, never more than three at any one time, and under cover of darkness.

The first reported incursions occurred on the night of 15-16 January when two Stukas each dropped an SC 1000 high-explosive bomb apiece on south-east London, and a third targeted Dover. Forty-eight hours later another trio raided the capital and two more returned the next night. Bad weather then halted operations. The Stukas next appeared shortly after sunrise on 5 February, an aircraft from 2./StG 1 attacking and sinking the RN trawler *Tourmaline* off the Kent coast, but paying the price by falling victim to a quartet of Spitfires of No 92 Sqn on convoy escort.

On the night of 11-12 February RN trawler *Eager* avenged her sister's loss by shooting down a 5.*Staffel* aircraft during a nocturnal dive bombing raid on Chatham naval dockyard. And the following night an aircraft of 9.*Staffel* failed to return from another such sortie over the Thames Estuary, although on this occasion no claims were made by the defenders – Feldwebel F Lewandowski and Unteroffizier L Rener simply being posted missing in 'J9+LL'.

This was the last reported loss of a Ju 87 over the United Kingdom. The early wartime career of a machine which had wreaked havoc from Warsaw to Dunkirk thus ended not with a bang, but with a whimper. Yet, even as the dark, wintry, waters of the Thames were closing over the black-bellied 'Berta' of 9./StG 1, the blue skies of the Mediterranean were witnessing a resurgence in the Stuka's fortunes. But that, as may have been said before, is another story . . .

Ju 87B-1, 'S2+UN' of 5./StG 77, which force-landed on Ham Manor Golf Course at Angmering, near Littlehampton, after the attack on Ford. Both crew members were seriously wounded by fire from the Spitfire I of No 602 Sqn's Sgt Basil Whall – the latter also went on to destroy a III./StG 77 machine, but was himself shot down in the process

ORDERS OF BATTLE

POLAND: 1 September 1939

***Luftflotte* 3** (Roth near Nuremberg): Gen der Flieger Hugo Sperrle

6. Fliegerdivision: Generalmajor Otto Dessloch

III./StG 51	Wertheim	Maj von Klitzing	Ju 87B	31-29

***Luftflotte* 1** (Stettin-Henningsholm): Gen der Flieger Albert Kesselring

1. Fliegerdivision: Generalleutnant Ulrich Grauert

II./StG 2	Stolp-Reitz	Haupt Schmidt	Ju 87B	35-34
III./StG 2	Stolp-West	Haupt Ott	Ju 87B	36-34
IV.(St)/LG 1	Stolp-Reitz	Haupt Kögel	Ju 87B	39-37
4.(St)/TrGr 186	Stolp-West	Haupt Blattner	Ju 87B/C	12-12

Luftwaffenkommando Ostpreußen: Generalleutnant Wilhelm Wimmer

I./StG 1	Elbing	Haupt Hozzel	Ju 87B	38-38

***Luftflotte* 4** (Reihenbach/Silesia): Gen der Flieger Alexander Löhr

2. *Fliegerdivision:* Generalmajor Bruno Loerzer

I./StG 2	Nieder-Ellguth	Maj Dinort	Ju 87B	38-37

Fliegerführer z.b.V: Generalmajor Wolfram *Freiherr* von Richthofen

Stab StG 77	Neudorf	Oberst Schwartzkopff	Ju 87B	3-3
I./StG 77	Ottmuth	Haupt von Dalwigk	Ju 87B	39-34
II./StG 77	Neudorf	Haupt von Schönborn	Ju 87B	39-38
I./StG 76	Nieder-Ellguth	Haupt Sigel	Ju 87B	36-28

THE LOW COUNTRIES AND FRANCE: 10 May 1940

***Luftflotte* 2** (Münster): Gen der Flieger Albert Kesselring

VIII. *Fliegerkorps*: Generalmajor *Freiherr* von Richthofen

Stab StG 2	Cologne-Ostheim	Maj Dinort	Ju 87B	3-3
I./StG 2	Cologne-Ostheim	Haupt Hitschhold	Ju 87B	40-23
III./StG 2	Nörvenich	Maj von Schönborn	Ju 87B	38-27
I./StG 76	Cologne-Ostheim	Haupt Sigel	Ju 87B	39-34
Stab StG 77	Cologne-Butzweilerhof	Oberst Schwartzkopff	Ju 87B	4-3
I./StG 77	Cologne-Butzweilerhof	Haupt von Dalwigk	Ju 87B	39-31
II./StG 77	Cologne-Butzweilerhof	Haupt Plewig	Ju 87B	39-30
IV.(St)/LG 1	Duisburg	Haupt Kösl	Ju 87B	39-37

***Luftflotte* 3** (Bad Orb): Gen der Flieger Hugo Sperrle

I. *Fliegerkorps:* Gen der Flieger Ulrich Grauert

III./StG 51	Cologne-Wahn	Maj von Klitzing	Ju 87B	39-31

II. *Fliegerkorps*: Generalleutnant Bruno Loerzer

Stab StG 1	Siegburg	Oberst Baier	Ju 87B	3-3
II./StG 2	Siegburg	Maj Enneccerus	Ju 87B	38-33
I.(St)/TrGr 186	Hemweiler	Haupt Hagen	Ju 87B	39-36

BATTLE OF BRITAIN: 13 August 1940

***Luftflotte* 2** (Brussels): Generalfeldmarschall Albert Kesselring

II. *Fliegerkorps:* Gen der Flieger Bruno Loerzer

II./StG 1 (III./StG 51)	Norrent-Fontès	Haupt Keil	Ju 87B	38-30
IV.(St)/LG 1	Tramecourt	Haupt von Brauchitsch	Ju 87B	36-28

***Luftflotte* 3** (Paris): Generalfeldmarschall Hugo Sperrle

VIII. *Fliegerkorps:* Gen der Flieger Wolfram von Richthofen

Stab StG 1	Angers	Maj Hagen	Ju 87B	3-2
I./StG 1	Angers	Maj Hozzel	Ju 87R	39-27
III./StG 1 (I.(St)/TrGr 186)	Angers	Haupt Mahlke	Ju 87B	38-26
Stab StG 2	St Malo	Maj Dinort	Ju 87B	4-3
I./StG 2	St Malo	Haupt Hitschhold	Ju 87B	35-29
II./StG 2	Lannion	Haupt Enneccerus	(Ju 87B	2-2)
			(Ju 87R	37-31)
III./StG 2	-	Haupt Brücker	Ju 87B	-
Stab StG 3	Caen	-	Ju 87B	5-2
I./StG3 (I./StG 76)	Caen	Haupt Sigel	Ju 87B	24-14
Stab StG 77	Caen	Maj von Schönborn	Ju 87B	4-3
I./StG 77	Caen	Haupt Meisel	Ju 87B	36-33
II./StG 77	Caen	-	Ju 87B	37-25
III./StG 77 (II./KG 76)	Caen	Haupt Bode	Ju 87B	38-37

STUKAGESCHWADER KNIGHT'S CROSS RECIPIENTS 1940

		Date of Award	Fate
1	Hozzel, Hauptmann Paul-Werner	8/5/40	
2	Möbus, Leutnant Martin	8/5/40	2/6/44 (+)
3	Schaefer, Oberleutnant Elmar	8/5/40	
4	Grenzel, Unteroffizier Gerhard	8/5/40	10/1/41 (MiA)
5	Dinort, Major Oskar	20/6/40	
6	von Dalwigk zu Lichtenfels, Hauptmann Friedrich-Karl *Freiherr*	21/7/40*	9/7/40 (KiA)
7	Enneccerus, Hauptmann Walter	21/7/40	
8	Hagen, Major Walter	21/7/40	
9	Hitschhold, Hauptmann Hubertus	21/7/40	
10	von Schönborn-Wiesentheid, Major Clemens *Graf*	21/7/40	30/8/44 (+)
11	Sigel, Hauptmann Walter	21/7/40	8/5/44 (+)
12	Keil, Hauptmann Anton	19/8/40	29/8/41 (KiA)
13	Brandenburg, Oberleutnant Johannes	18/9/40	28/2/42 (KiA)
14	Schwartzkopff, Oberst Gunther	24/11/40*	14/5/40 (KiA)
15	Plewig, Hauptmann Waldemar	14/12/40	8/8/40 (PoW)

*posthumous (+) killed whilst on active service

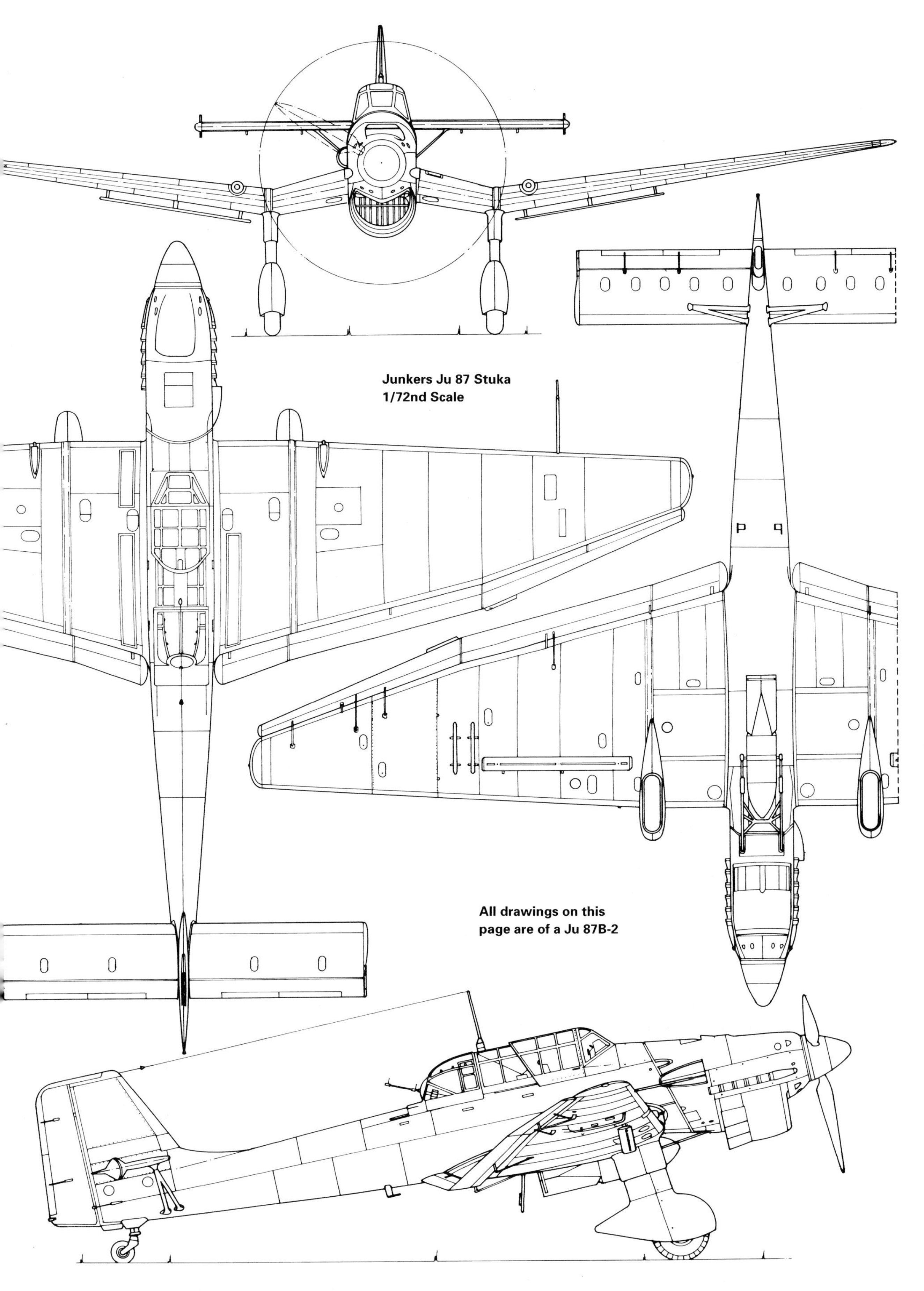
Junkers Ju 87 Stuka
1/72nd Scale
All drawings on this
page are of a Ju 87B-2

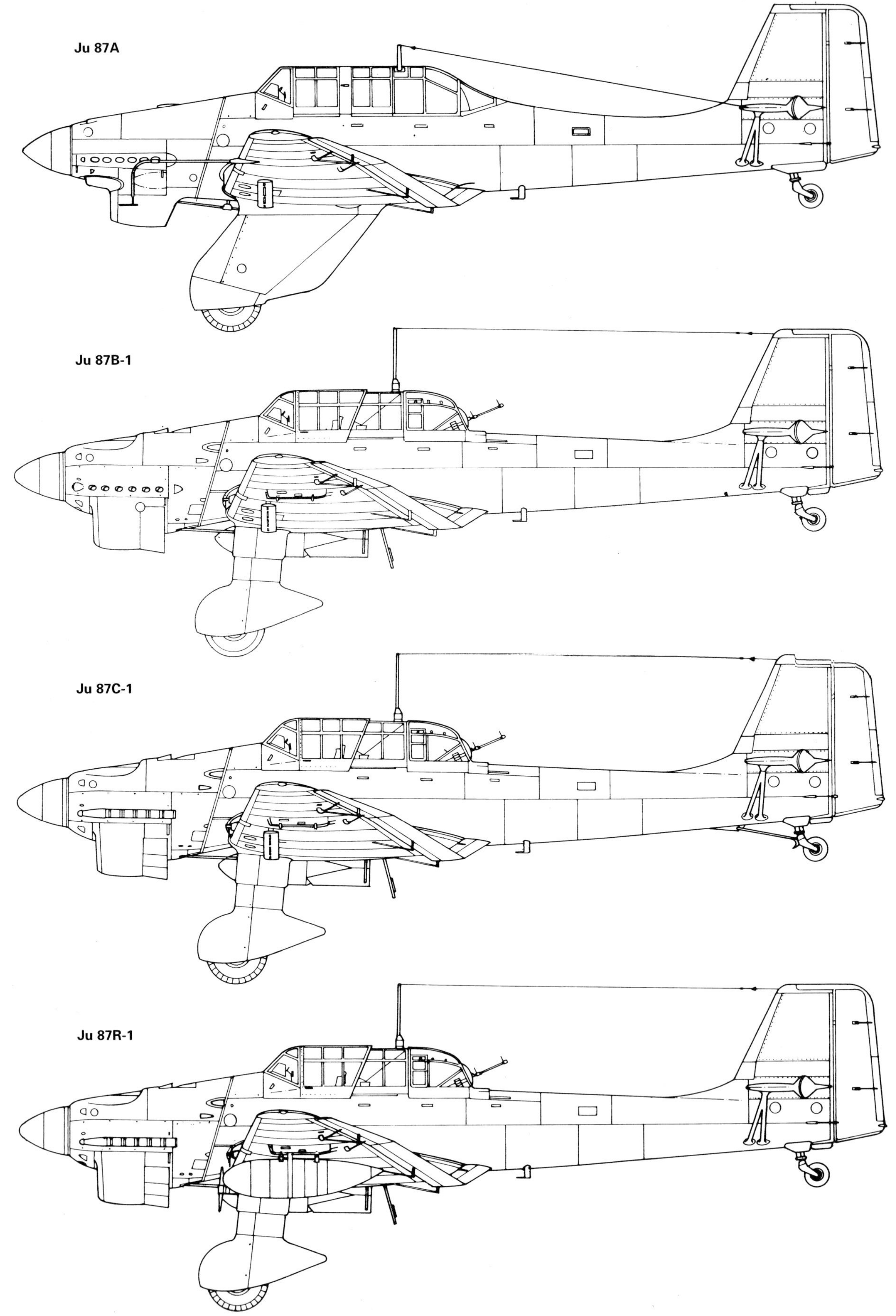
Ju 87A
Ju 87B-1
Ju 87C-1
Ju 87R-1